DEMAND
EXCELLENCE

On and Off the Field

Jonathan Gess

DEMAND EXCELLENCE: ON AND OFF THE FIELD
Copyright © 2019 by Jonathan Gess

Library of Congress Control Number: 2018957886
ISBN-13:   Paperback: 978-1-64398-373-8
            PDF: 978-1-64398-374-5
            ePub: 978-1-64398-375-2
            Kindle: 978-1-64398-376-9

Printed in the United States of America

LitFire LLC
1-800-511-9787
www.litfirepublishing.com
order@litfirepublishing.com

CONTENTS

DEDICATION

TO THE PLAYERS I HAVE coached and will coach: You know I love you! You are a blessing to me and you always know I am in the weight room if you need anything! Pursue Christ with all diligence! Be men for Jesus Christ.

To my beautiful wife Dee: I love you and am thankful for you! You deserve better than me but thank you for putting up with me. To see the Godly woman you have grown into over the past 17 years is proof of God's goodness. I am blessed.

Uriah: You are a blessing! Your mom and my diligent prayer for you is that you become a man for Jesus Christ. Your mom and I love you!

To my mom and dad: I have only the fondest memories and know I was loved. You taught me Jesus Christ and demanded I go to church even when I was married. You are my greatest supporters even now. Dad, you hurt worse than I hurt when we lose! I am forever grateful! I love you.

To my Christian Brothers and Sisters out there: May we live daily to advance the Gospel of Jesus Christ.

PREFACE

I LAY THERE WIDE AWAKE with my heart pounding. I threw the covers off because I was sweating profusely. I was having a nightmare—a horrible nightmare! We were getting beat. Maybe we had lost. I can't figure out which. But it is awful. I come to my senses, and I am relieved. It is just a dream!

This occurred in summer 2018 when my family and I were on vacation. Isn't vacation supposed to be relaxing and a time we can get away from the stress and worry of life? My goodness, what is my problem? Why am I this way? We had won thirty-six games in a row, and we had won three state championships in a row. We had won four state championships since 2012. Surely, I could be at peace and relax. Just a little bit of peace!

But it was the opposite. I was as restless as I had ever been in my life. I was praying to the Lord for peace and that my mind would be still. In fact, if you looked in my journal where I write my prayers, you would see the word FREEDOM written all over the place. But I wasn't getting freedom. I was in bondage. This was my prayer for freedom: "Please, Lord, remove this from me. Give me rest and peace in you. I lay down this sinful desire to be the best down at your feet."

And this is the war of a football coach, the war between our souls being enslaved to success against the pursuit of godliness. This war is between pursuing the approval of the world and man against pursuing the approval of our Lord and Savior, Jesus Christ. It has haunted me since playing college football, has followed me into the Air Force, and has enslaved me as a head football coach. What to do?

I went back and started reading the book I wrote after the 2013 season. I had been a head coach for seven seasons and had many failures and many successes. God had taken me through a journey, and I clearly saw what a Christian football coach was supposed to look like. I wrote it all down as a philosophy on how to put Christ first in the pursuit of winning football games. It also serves as a great foundation for building a great culture within a football program or any organization. As I read it, I was amazed at the struggle God had brought me through back then and how I was going through the same thing once again. But going through the book helped center me on some core beliefs I have as a football coach.

I didn't publish the book back then when I wrote it because I was unsure if it would help anyone or if anyone would even want something written by a thirty-four-year-old. So it set in a computer file for the past five years until I returned to it due to my struggle. I am now thirty-nine, and it seems like I know more coaches younger than me than I do coaches older than me.

I have enjoyed my time with our current defensive coordinator, Brett Collier. He is very much like me. He wants to be the best, but he wants to honor God as well. I know the battle that rages in his soul is the same war that battles in my soul. Brett is going to be a head coach one day, and I hope to help lay a foundation in him to where this game will not chew him up and spit him out. I want him to understand his first duties are a husband and father before he is a football coach. But that is easier said than done. I pray that he will grow strong in relationship with Jesus Christ as football coach and not grow cold and distant from his ultimate purpose—to glorify God through being a great husband, a great dad, and coaching young men in the game of football. I think there are many other guys like Brett out there who would enjoy this book.

You men who are older than me—I can't decide if you will read this or not. You will see my struggle and either laugh or connect. You laugh at my naivety and foolishness of wrestling with the god of success, as life experiences have shown you it cannot be conquered. You cannot conquer success because there is always more to be had. It never ends. You laugh at this game we play with success. However, you may connect with me because you are right there with me even though you are older than me. You might be forty-nine, fifty-nine, or even sixty-nine and you are still struggling and toiling with the god of winning. This book is for you as we battle together.

Before we get going with this book, I know I mentioned we are coming off a thirty-six-game win streak. It has not always been so pretty. I wrote this book in 2013, and we were coming off a five-year 48–5 run. Guess what happened in 2014? We started the year off 0–6. Those were trying times, but we kept the faith. We believed in our "Win the Day" philosophy (it's a chapter in the book), and we just kept at it.

Once we hit region play, we were able to win all our games and make the playoffs. We got lucky and got in the easier playoff bracket. We rolled through the playoffs and made the state championship game—only to get destroyed! As I mention in this book that the 2011 state semifinal loss was the worst loss of my life (still is). That 49–7 beatdown we took in the 2014 state championship game was the most embarrassing.

But you know what is amazing? After that 7–7 season and that embarrassing loss, I wasn't waking up in cold sweats dreaming about losing. Shoot, I just lived it out. I didn't fear losing; I just experienced the worst loss ever and lived to tell about it! I was excited about the new season and getting to redeem ourselves. I was not living in dread we may lose. I was *free*!

I mention that just to let you know I've been embarrassed and I've questioned why in the world I coach this game (almost daily). I've had many people tell me I'm not a good coach or that I don't do this or that right. That I shouldn't take every snap in shotgun or I run the ball too much. That I run to the right too much and that I don't take enough chances. There will always be critics telling you how to do your job. I have had to learn on the fly how to lead grown men and how to set expectations for our program. I had to learn to be bold in what I believe will win and confidently pursue excellence in those beliefs.

God led me in many ways. If you allow him, God will lead you. It is true: "He who calls you is faithful; he will surely do it" (1 Thess. 5:24, ESV). So stay at it. "Keep Choppin'," as we say at my school.

Finally, I want to thank God for the good things he has done. He has given me a wife who loves the Lord, and God is giving her more and more wisdom each and every day as she is diligent to pursue Christ. This impacts a man a great deal and is a gift from the Lord. He has placed me in a school where the leadership loves the Lord and they influence me and hold me accountable to be a better Christian. Over the years, the parents of the players I coach are successful professionals from whom I have learned so much from about leadership and how to run a program. I must say it again: "He who calls you is faithful; he will surely do it."

So I am publishing this book. And I hope it helps you, as it helps me, to shine as a light for Jesus Christ, "that you may be blameless and innocent, children of God without blemish in the midst of a crooked and twisted generation, among whom you shine as lights in the world" (Phil. 2:15, ESV).

INTRODUCTION

THIS BOOK IS WRITTEN FOR guys like me—men who love the Lord and want to be the very best at what they do, those who have an insatiable desire to excel. I found balancing serving the Lord with my whole heart and seeking to be the absolute best at what I do impossible. What I have found out over the years is, it is impossible. One is going to take precedent over the other. If I want to be a man who serves the Lord with my whole heart, nothing can be balanced with this. However, I do believe God has given me this insatiable desire to win and will use it for his purpose as I make him my purpose. This whole process I call being a Champion for Jesus Christ. It is all about getting our priorities in order.

I'm a high school football coach, and I want to win. I want to win at anything I do. I'm always looking for the best way to coach, to inspire, and to lead. Like many coaches, I will spend many hours tweaking our practice schedule so no time is wasted. I am consumed with executing flawlessly and developing the perfect process to ensure success on game day. I demand perfection from myself, from our players, and from the coaches with whom I work, all for the ultimate goal of winning a championship. Like many of you reading this book, I want to be number

1 when the final whistle blows! I've been second place, and I am not okay with it. It bothers me. I want to be a champion! And this is where I find myself in a great paradox between serving God and serving self.

The world's definition of *champion* is being the absolute best. This must be proven through competition. I completely agree with this. (And, yes, throughout this book, I will identify a worldly champion with a lowercase *c* and Champion for Jesus Christ with a capital *C*). However, I think God views being a Champion a little different. I believe we are Champions for Jesus Christ when we give our absolute best to maximize the talent God has given us for his glory and his purposes. Being a Champion cannot be and is not a onetime event. It is a daily process and pursuit. Each day you either win or you lose. This is true in our professional lives and our pursuit of Jesus Christ. In fact, I think you cannot separate the two. Can you be a champion in your professional life and yet not a champion in your Spiritual life? Does this make you half a champion? Being a Champion for Christ is making Christ central in all our endeavors and letting him shine through us.

As I talk through this book, I am going to refer most of the time to situations in my life and use *I* a lot. However, we are all Christian brothers in pursuit of the same goal—being Champions for Jesus Christ. We are all one. As I wrote this book, I was thinking about the players I've coached and how I could motivate them to live their lives with their eyes focused on Christ. I think about other coaches who have the opportunity to live for Christ in front of their player's daily and, through this, make an impact on them for eternity. I think about men who are leaders in the community and in the workplace. I think about the men who are fathers. As followers of Jesus Christ, we are all one, and we all have the same goal! So when I say "I," I'm writing to you and me!

I'm a coach so I'm writing from a coaching viewpoint. Therefore, I'm going to make references to coaching and coaches a lot. I think any man who is a leader of men is a coach. I may lead on the football field and you may lead in an assortment of different positions. A coach's job is to lead, instruct, and inspire men to work together to accomplish a goal. With that definition, everyone is a coach. The ideas in this book are challenges God has laid on my heart in my own life as a coach of young men. I am never speaking at or down to anyone. Every word is a challenge first and foremost to me. I fail daily. I am a sinner saved by the grace of our Lord, Jesus Christ.

God has called each of us to live as Champions. Champions live to impact the world for Jesus Christ. What if we all viewed ourselves as coaches for Jesus Christ and winning a championship was defined as building God's kingdom? As we stand before men and lead them, we must understand their value is not in the ability to win a worldly game; it is to be men and women who reflect God's glory and his radiance. We are to pursue excellence only because it will bring glory to Jesus Christ, not ourselves. We are to work to maximize our talents in order to be fruitful for the kingdom of God. We must warn the people we influence how they can gain the whole world and yet lose their soul. We must instruct them how to lose the world and win eternity.

Keep Your Eyes on Christ

As a Christian coach I cannot let the world dictate to me what the words *win, championship,* and *champion* mean. I must live for a much higher purpose than the perishable trophy we will receive for winning a game here on earth. As 1 Corinthians 9:24–25 says, "Do you not know that in a race all the runners run, but only one receives the prize? So run that you may obtain it. Every athlete exercises self-control in all things. They do it to receive a perishable wreath, but we an imperishable."

We must set our minds on Christ as we lead. The world teaches lies to the young men I coach by leading them to believe that ultimate satisfaction comes from the pursuit of a dream and then the realization of that dream. We all fall prey to this. Too many worldly champions in their sport are losers in all that is important to Jesus Christ. Coaches must define to their players what real winning is. What good is it that a man win a national championship yet is a complete failure as a leader in his home and in the community? As men whom God has called into the lives of these young men, we must change the purpose of the game. We must change the objective of the game, and in doing so, God will use us to transform the next generation of leaders.

I have laid out the structure of this book almost exactly how God has inspired me to lead for him. Each year that I have coached, God has laid certain ideas on my heart. He first unveiled my eyes to the fact that being a coach was to be for his glory and to build his kingdom rather than serve my own interests. Once I surrendered everything to the Lord, God really started to direct my steps in an overall philosophy in how I should lead young men. I enjoyed writing in detail about each idea, and I was convicted reading back through what God placed upon my heart. I hope you find these ideas helpful. I pray God continue to raise up men who will lead for Jesus Christ!

A Prayer

Each chapter will end with a prayer.

> How great you are, my God and my King. You are the Creator of the heavens and the earth. You have created me from the dust of the earth; my heart beats because you will it. You are my Sustainer; health and life are in your hands. I am a sinner and in desperate need of a Savior. You have saved my soul through the blood of Jesus Christ. I do not fear death because you have destroyed its grip on me through the death and resurrection of Jesus Christ. I once was separated from God but now have access to the Father through the work of Jesus Christ. I

once had no hope for the future but now look forward to eternity with Christ.

O Lord, help me to lead these young men I coach for the kingdom of Jesus Christ. May it be your glory and your kingdom I pursue excellence and not for my own glory. I praise you for the joy of competition. I love the fun in the pursuit of winning a championship in the game I coach. But, Lord, never let this be my identity or my priority. May I always seek you and your kingdom first! May I be totally surrendered to you. May my life bring you glory and honor. Amen.

1

DEMAND EXCELLENCE

EXCELLENCE IS SEEKING TO BRING God glory and honor by giving perfect effort to become your absolute best with the talent God has given you in *all* that God has called you to do. A *Winner* is someone who wakes up each day in the pursuit of excellence. A *Champion* is a person who perseveres with unwavering commitment, longing to hear these words promised from our Father: "Well done, good and faithful servant. You have been faithful over a little; I will set you over much. Enter into the joy of your master" (Matt. 25:21, ESV).

It is imperative I define words correctly. My whole goal is be a Champion and to create Champions. The pursuit of excellence and winning will produce Champions. I believe the key words in the definition of excellence are "in *all* God has called you to do." These young men I coach are called to perform in school academically, honor their father and mother, serve the Lord with their bodies, lead for Christ in school, and excel as athletes. Pursuing all these is excellence. As they look back over the whole year and they were successful in persevering, then they are Champions in the eyes of Christ.

This world glorifies men and women who have had great success on the field or in the arena yet are losers as husbands or wives, mothers or fathers, and leaders for Christ in the community. It is not hard to become the best at the sport you play if God has given you amazing ability and you work at it. However, it is hard to pursue excellence as an athlete, a father, a husband, and a leader in the community for Jesus Christ. Being excellent on the field or in the arena without pursuing excellence in the areas that are important to God is being a loser. Therefore, excellence should be a term used for men who seek to do well in all aspects of their life, not just the one that will get them worldly glory!

What is important to me will be important to my players. If I make winning the game our main objective, then my players will do the same. If I teach our players that excellence on the field is important but secondary to pursuing Christlike character, hopefully, my players will focus on this. This is no easy task: the world and our flesh make winning on the field the only purpose of any value or importance. I will not be praised by the world for teaching our young men and women to put on Christ and become like him. But I must remember, I do not serve the world—I serve Jesus Christ. My goal is to be a Champion for Jesus Christ, not this world. I must Demand Excellence in this area from myself, if I am going to instruct my players on this path.

What Does Excellence Look Like?

What does excellence look like in the eyes of Christ? I want to give a description of a football practice I believe would glorify our Lord. Coaches are coaching hard and get on their players but do so in a spirit of love, motivation, and encouragement. The players love and respect their coaches. This relationship has been forged through the coaches and players interacting off the field together in a loving and nurturing environment. The coaches have the right to challenge and push the players because they have poured into them over the course of the off-season athletically and spiritually. There is no profanity or demeaning talk from either player or coaches. The coaches are unified in their quest to produce the best players and the best men for Christ. The players are humble and obedient as instruction and commands are issued. The players are hungry to improve and know coaching and instruction are the key components to success.

As these young men have been trained in excellence on the practice field, it translates over the game field. The players play with a relentless desire to excel as they play for their brothers and their coaches. They do not play for self-glorification but give all and sacrifice all for the glory of the team. They play with a desire that is unmatched because they play for a purpose much greater than themselves. Even though they play with relentless resolve, they do not do so with malicious intent against their competitors. They are consumed with their own performance and desire to do the very best they can because this is the objective of a competitor.

In victory, the team is humble as they honor their teammates, their opponents, and, most importantly, Jesus Christ. In defeat, the team is gracious and looks to honor the great performance of their competitors. Instead of looking around for someone to blame, each player and coach will look to what they could have done to improve the outcome of the game from a loss to a victory. Under no circumstance do players put their heads down and sulk and feel sorry for themselves. This is not the attitude of a Winner or a Champion. They hold their head high, looking forward to the opportunity to improve the next day. One loss never defines a man. The desire to improve in response to a loss is what creates a Champion!

These same coaches and players who demand excellence on the field are leaders off the field. The coaches are focused on being faithful husbands, loving fathers, and desire to impact people in the community for Jesus Christ. The players are young men who take ownership in the classroom and are respectful to authority. They lead their peers in the right way and do not swerve from being lights for Jesus Christ on the weekends. They are men of *integrity*, which is being faithful to live for Jesus Christ no matter the place, situation, or circumstance.

An Example of a Man of Excellence

In 2011, we were all set to play a home game the first game of the season against a team we had previously traveled to play in Florida in 2010. It is very hard to find a football game when everyone has a full schedule. We were searching all around and our athletic director, Coach Scott Queen, decided to send an email to Fred Yancey at Briarwood Christian Academy. I thought, *Are you kidding me? I just watched those guys on TV a few years before, and I know Briarwood has been a powerhouse in class AAAAA in Alabama. There is no way we need to play anyone who has been on TV.* I figured our AD was trying to get me fired, crazy, or both.

In my head, I had concocted an idea of how an amazing football coach is supposed to look, act, and talk. They were supposed to carry themselves with arrogance and look down upon everyone else. Yes, of course, they would have an appearance of humility; but I just knew, when I looked into their eyes, I would not be able to measure up. Championship coaches were made of something I couldn't conceive. So when Coach Queen told me to call Coach Yancey and talk with him about it, I was extremely intimidated.

I mustered up the courage to call Coach Yancey and was shocked beyond belief. Here I was talking to a championship football coach, a coach of one of the top teams in the state of Alabama year in and year out, and he was one of the most humble and caring men with whom I had ever talked. He never talked about himself, he never boasted all his accomplishments, and he constantly told me we were a good football team. I could tell there was something different about this man.

I agreed to play him, and I hung up the phone. Five minutes later, I sat there and this thought ran my mind: *Jonathan, you are an idiot, a sucker! Coach Yancey buttered you up, and he knows he has a loaded team. He just wanted an easy win, and he tricked you into thinking you can actually play with him. You are a fool!* I was ready to get up and go yell at Coach Queen. Man, how did I get myself into this?

Yes, I understood we were going to have to play bigger and better teams if we were going to continue to grow as a football program, but the team who just lost in the AAAAA Alabama state championship game? We just lost in the class A Georgia quarterfinals. And to make matters worse, they had 19 returning starters. And, oh yeah, my team was going to field 68 players. They had 120, 40 of which were seniors.

I was getting my resume ready; surely, our headmaster was going to get rid of me after this game as I was leading my team to the slaughter. Coach Queen would be fired too, right? He got me into this mess!

Let me fast-forward through all the nervous breakdowns I would go through during the summer watching film of Briarwood. I don't even know why coaches exchange film so early in the summer. All it does is give us time to overanalyze and stress out. Either way, game week verse Briarwood approached, and we worked hard to develop a good game plan. I had good players too, and I knew it. I just didn't have the army Coach Yancey was bringing!

Game day approached, and I was excited to meet this legend of a coach. I had never seen Coach Yancey, and I figured he would be about six foot four and one of the most intimidating men I had ever seen. I completely forgot the phone conversations we had where he seemed so gentle, kind, and peaceful. I think that is because I would keep turning on the game film and seeing a small army on the field. I had never seen such a well-coached defense. I could not figure out how we were going to get a yard.

Game day arrived, and Briarwood made it to our campus and unloaded the buses. I was scouring through what seemed like 300 football players walking the field looking for this larger-than-life man I had concocted in my head. I found him, and he was nothing as I suspected. Coach Yancey is an older man, probably around 60, maybe

5'11", and maybe 175 pounds. To this day, he was one of the nicest and most humble men I have ever met. As I talked to this man, I could sense the Holy Spirit living in him. Before me stood a man who I knew the Lord had used in mighty ways as a football coach.

I picked Coach Yancey's brain for a while, and I remember one topic I just had to discuss with him: "Coach Yancey, how in the world do you not play your best skill players and linemen both ways?"

Coach Yancey very humbly looked at the ground and said, "You know, I just have found that if you don't play your kids both ways, you always have a chance to win the game in the fourth quarter. The other team may have more talent, but it will all equal out in the second half. If you can just hang around with a more talented team and be willing to go in losing at halftime, you will have a chance to win in the fourth quarter."

In that statement, Coach Yancey became a prophet in my eyes. I had a talented team, but I made all of those kids play both ways. We were up 19–7 at the half, but those talented players I had were all throwing up, cramping up, or on IVs at halftime. Coach Yancey and his team pulled out the victory with 21–19 with the final score coming under 2 minutes to go in the fourth quarter. What a valuable lesson I learned that night: you don't have to play your best players on both sides of the ball all night! In fact, you can't!

I tell this story because Coach Yancey built a successful football program putting Christ first. It was the first time in my life I had witnessed a Christ-centered man who had won at the highest high school football level. He was gentle, humble, and kind. He was not overbearing. He did not think too much of himself. He invested all of himself into his football players. He loved them, and they loved him.

God would use this encounter with Coach Yancey in so many ways in my life going forward. For one, in 2012, I made a commitment to not playing kids both ways as much as possible, and we would win the state championship. I learned to be at peace with letting Christ live through me. Coach Yancey certainly did not care what the world had to say about being gentle, kind, and humble. He was comfortable in who he was as a coach. He was comfortable in Christ. He was an example of what excellence looked like as a coach in my eyes. He was a Champion both on the field and off the field. I prayed God would make me more like Coach Yancey who seemed to care way more about his players and Christ than he did himself.

Jesus—the Example of Excellence

I have just described excellence as a competitor. This is the standard, and as coaches, we must demand this. As we demand excellence from our players so they may be Champions for Jesus Christ, we must understand that some days we will fail. There are many ways a coach can fail and respond incorrectly. However, we must be quick to humble ourselves and ask for forgiveness from our players, coaches, and parents. We do and will mess up. Being strong enough to admit our failure and apologize for it will go a long way in promoting an attitude of excellence among our players.

In order to ask for forgiveness and admit where we are wrong, it requires humility. The first requirement for excellence in how it has been defined is humility. We must count ourselves as insignificant and count others as more important. There is no greater example in the world of excellence, winning, and a champion than Jesus Christ:

> Do nothing from selfish ambition or conceit, but in humility count others more significant than yourselves. Let each of you look not only to his own interests, but also to the interests of others. Have this mind among yourselves, which is yours in Christ Jesus, who, though he was in the form of God, did not count equality with God a thing to be grasped, but emptied himself, by taking the form of a servant, being

born in the likeness of men. And being found in human form, he humbled himself by becoming obedient to the point of death, even death on a cross. Therefore God has highly exalted him and bestowed on him the name that is above every name, so that at the name of Jesus every knee should bow, in heaven and on earth and under the earth, and every tongue confess that Jesus Christ is Lord, to the glory of God the Father (Phil. 2:3–11, ESV).

In context with excellence, Christ gave perfect effort and became the absolute best for us while he was on earth. His absolute best was suffering and dying on the cross for our sins so we may have eternal life. Each day he was on earth, he died to the desires of this world and won for the kingdom of God. And when his time was up and he had finished the work God gave him, he became the Champion over sin and death. Christ is now our Champion, and we can become Champions in him. In this pursuit, we must Demand Excellence!

A Prayer

How great you are, O Lord, my King! There is no higher standard of excellence than you. There is no greater example of a Champion than Jesus Christ.

As we seek to be leaders for Jesus Christ, help us to keep our eyes on you and building your kingdom. Help us to seek the things that are above, where Christ is—seated at the right hand of God. May we set our minds on the things that are above, not on the things that are on earth.

Lord, may we have no desire for perishable trophies and the fleeting glory given by man. No, may we set our eyes upon you and seek only your approval. Help us to die to our sinful selves and may we live in Christ.

Fill us with your Holy Spirit and lead us in the way everlasting. May we long for the glory that will come upon your return. Our glory is in Jesus Christ; help us live for this purpose each day. To you be all the honor and glory! Amen.

2

THE MISSION

THE MISSION OF OUR FOOTBALL program is real simple: to build Champions for Jesus Christ. There is a big difference in pursuing winning championships in comparison to building Champions for Christ. God is not really concerned with how many championships we win as coaches, but he is concerned with how many Champions we work to build. As you look at the mission and reflect on the mission, it seems very simple. However, if you are competitive and have a desire to win games, you will constantly battle your flesh in making this the number one objective as a coach.

I Started to Bow at the Feet of Winning

We have to win a championship, was the badgering thought in my subconscious. In 2009, we had a great team that could score points in droves, but we got knocked out of the second round 46–39. The year before that, 2008, we lost 7–0 in the second round. Then in 2010, we had the magical team, only to get knocked out in the quarterfinals 35–29 by the team that would eventually become the state champion. I just couldn't lead my team to victory in the big playoff games. I knew to keep working, but I had doubts.

I didn't really know what to expect in the 2011 season. We had a ton of talent returning, but we just lost four Division I football players. I couldn't win a state championship with four Division I football players the year before, so I had little confidence I could do it with a team that boasted two. Don't get me wrong, though, I'm always going to work and do my very best; I just didn't know what our best was going to be in 2011.

After the loss to Briarwood, we got on a roll. *Just maybe we have a state championship football team this year*, I began to allow myself to think. We had a lot of things we had to improve on each week, but we certainly were playing well and had a chance to win it all. We did improve each week, and we got better and better. Our eyes became firmly fixed on the prize—the state championship. The coaches worked hard, and the players practiced hard. *We are going to do it. We are going to win the state championship this year*, we were all thinking it!

I'm not ignorant. I know you don't discuss those things out loud. As a coach, I am to direct the eyes and the hearts of my players at the task at hand each particular week. My greatest error, though, was that I did not warn everyone of the consequences of pride and arrogance creeping in. I didn't see it creeping in. I allowed my team and coaches to set their eyes on the state championship. I did not warn of the importance of humility. Pride and arrogance slowly crept in, and by the end of the season, I had an uncontrollable beast. I didn't even know its dangers.

What I realized later is I slowly through previous years started to let my ability to win games define me as a person. After all, I was a football coach, and a coach's identity and value to this world is in how many games he can win. I became obsessed with winning. I wanted to be the best coach in the world. The De La Salle coach won something crazy like 150 games in a row, so I needed to beat this! I was figuring it all out. The three previous years were all learning experiences for me. I had been through the adversity, through the fire, I was going to lead our team to a state championship that year. God had put me through all that adversity so I could make it happen that year. I had been forged through fire. I was ready.

Even though I loved the Lord, this lust for winning was taking me over. I was allowing my identity to be defined in being able to will my team to victory. I was being pulled from my identity in Christ. I didn't see it. I praise God, for when he saves us, he does not lose his grip on us. I was drifting, but God had a firm grasp on me.

Let Christ Lead

The head coach likes to think the team they coach is theirs. Through the power of the Holy Spirit, you have to surrender the team you coach to God. My team and my players are not a source of pride or a way in which I seek glory or to be used by me to help me advance my career. I pray God empowers me to coach in a way that I am influencing our team, parents, and fans for the glory of Jesus Christ. I pray I continue to surrender all to Christ. In surrendering all to Christ, he becomes my source of strength and power. He becomes my teacher and my counselor: "I will instruct and teach you in the way you should go; I will counsel you with my eye upon you" (Ps. 32:8, ESV).

Can there be any more powerful verse in scripture than Psalm 32:8? The Lord is promising us that he will instruct us and teach us in the way we should go. The King of the universe, the Creator of all things, the Savior, omnipotent and sovereign—he promises to lead us. He will counsel us through his Word and his Holy Spirit living inside of us. I pray this prayer daily: "Lord, instruct me and teach me in the way I should go. Counsel me today as I make decisions and influence people." I know the Lord is the author of knowledge and insight. Knowledge and insight from God leads to wisdom, discernment, discretion, and prudence. I desire all these!

As Christians here on this earth, we will always have to battle our flesh. I have many battles in which I have to engage; the pursuit of winning at all costs is a major one. Apart from Christ, I know I would pursue winning with unparalleled passion. Winning would become the focus of my mind, body, and spirit. In my sinful flesh, I desire this! However, I realize all that is important to Christ would suffer if worldly winning were my number 1 focus. For example, God first cares that I am a faithful husband and a loving and present father. The lust for winning has no room for wives and children.

The lust of winning also completely distorts the view I have of the kids I coach. Instead of being young men made in the image of God for his glory and honor, they now become products upon which I can build glory and fame for myself while advancing my career. I know that seems harsh, but it is the truth. When we make winning championships our most valued possession, we have created an idol.

Winning as an Idol

When I first starting coaching, I would sell to my parents that we were going to do two things simultaneously: (1) win and (2) we will build young boys into godly young men. I felt good about this mission, but winning quickly started to become an idol and my source of pride. Through challenging circumstances, I was convicted by scripture: "No one can serve two masters, for either he will hate the one and love the other, or he will be devoted to the one and despise the other" (Matt. 6:24, ESV).

Plain and simple, I could not make building godly men and pursue winning at the same time. The worldly idol of winning can cause me to not place the souls of young men first. I had to reprioritize my mission. I could not (and cannot) let the idol of winning football games interfere with the kingdom mission of building young men for Christ. I was either going to become a coach who used the game of football to glorify and exalt myself, or I was going to become a man who used the game to impact others for Jesus Christ. In my natural, sinful state, I would choose to exalt myself every time. But, praise the Lord, the Holy Spirit was working in me and driving me to kill the desire for self-glorification.

A great example of how the god of winning can destroy our joy comes from my fifth year as a head football coach. After I had been a head coach for a few years, I started to develop my mission and my process of doing things. As I mentioned, I thought I was so wise and that my mission would be to (1) win and (2) build men for Jesus Christ. I would sell this to parents, coaches, players, and administrators.

In the first few years, we built a good program, and we did win. I do think we impacted many for Christ. However, the lust of winning started to destroy the joy I had in football. The pride of winning started to destroy players, coaches, and parents. Football and winning had quickly become the priority. It was obvious—the mission of building champions for Jesus Christ was secondary.

Sin is subtle and sneaky. It creeps in, and you don't even realize it. Over the course of time, this obsession with winning finally started to destroy my joy in coaching. In 2011, I was miserable even though we were winning. We would win by forty but not be happy because we didn't dominate enough. I don't know if I carried myself in a prideful and arrogant way, but I was losing control of my expectations and how I treated my players. Instead of loving, motivating, and encouraging them, I started to bark and harp on them. I developed unrealistic expectations for them. And when you develop unrealistic expectations, you become irrational. Winning was not enough anymore; dominating was the new goal.

Praise God that he will destroy pride in us and get us back on track. Coming off a 51–7 victory in the third round of the playoffs against a team we thought could beat us, we entered into the semifinals against a team we had already beaten in the season. Yes, everyone was thinking we will be dominating this opponent, and we were a lock for the state championship game. The previous two games, we had dominated like the coaches expected, and we felt really good about ourselves. We knew we were going to the state championship game, and we were not worried about winning the semifinal game; we were consumed with dominating the semifinal game. More glory for us!

Guess what? We got beat 14–7 in the semifinals. I can honestly say this was the worst loss in my life. This was my most embarrassing moment ever. You know why? My whole identity had become winning. I was humiliated. This marked the beginning of God's destroying the idol of winning from my life.

I do not want anyone to think that there was any big sin in my life I was committing or that we completely did not use football as a tool to preach Christ. We did preach Christ, and I was pursuing him. Still, though, my priorities were not in line, and we were drifting from our mission through the game of football. Winning became our primary focus and Christ was second. We didn't mean for this to happen, but it is what happens when you try to serve two masters (Matt. 6:24). It was my fault. I was the head coach.

The Mission

Over the few months after this game, God really started to reveal to me that I needed to be much more intentional in my mission to build young men into men for Jesus Christ. (I now call this building Champions for Jesus Christ.) He made it crystal clear to me that we cannot pursue championships as our number 1 focus. We must be wholly committed to building Champions for Jesus Christ. I needed to by wholly committed to his cause! Once again, it's not that we were not focused on this as a program, but my thoughts and priorities had gotten off-kilter. Instead of being consumed with defensive yards given up, points given up, or points scored—all areas of pride—I needed to start keeping tabs on the hearts of the young men placed under my tutelage by the Lord.

It was a rather simple yet complex change that had to be made. The Lord was clearly telling me that my mission was to invest in the souls of young men for Jesus Christ. Through this process, God would use us to build Champions for him. There was no room for my selfish agenda. More importantly, there was no room for me! God had called me into coaching to preach Christ to everyone and anyone who came along my path. I am a servant no longer seeking any glory for myself. Football is a tool to be used to build Champions for Christ—simple yet complicated!

As I let go of the god of winning, I found freedom in my life. I still have stress and anxiety in the preparation but not in the winning. And please don't get me wrong—I'm still a very intense competitor who wants to win. I'm not weak and I'm not soft, and I loathe those who are. In fact, this whole process and perspective has just made the process of seeking to win more fun. There is now eternal value in seeking to win football games. Winning and being a champion has been redefined. My focus is now on the souls of the young men I coach and being an example for them. Win or lose, I love them, and I believe they are champions, whether they win on the football field or not.

Operation G220

All this mission talk sounds so good, but you must fight and battle to keep Christ your number 1 focus. We are sinful people, and we lust and desire things we should not. If I am going to keep Christ at the center of the program and be effective in my mission of building Champions for Jesus Christ, I must be very intentional each season so I do not slowly drift.

To keep my mind mission focused each year since 2012, I have developed an operation theme. In 2012 our theme was Operation G220. This came from Galatians 2:20. In 2013, it was Operation J330. This came from John 3:30. As you read these verses, you will see they discuss making oneself nothing and making Christ everything. Some people may think this is stupid and the stuff nerds would do. The world will think this for sure. If I let the world influence the decisions I make in leading the young men God has given me, I will never do anything for the glory of God. I must keep my eyes on Christ and not the world.

Notice I do not start the season off with "Operation Win a State Championship." This will happen if we take care of our business, and God allows it to happen. Our main focus is humbly serving Jesus Christ. Coaches and players have different roles in this process. However, as the head coach, I will set the priorities, and it starts with properly addressing the overall year-in-and-year-out mission of your program and then yearly focusing the minds and hearts of all the players, coaches, and fans on the mission.

Strength in Christ

The world looks at all we have just discussed and will laugh and mock, thinking that it is a sign of weakness. Losers wouldn't make being number 1 or winning a championship the ultimate goal. I do not serve the world nor do I care what the world has to say. I set my eyes upon Christ and heaven and seek to bring glory to the one who created me, sustains me, and has given to me salvation. He is my Strength, my Hope, and my Trust. When I take my eyes off him and when I do not seek him, I am weak and the world has its appeal. But I know to set my eyes back on Christ.

This world and all that it has to offer is dying, but Christ is eternal. I stay focused on the mission and do not listen to the mocking of the scoffers in this world. There is only one imperishable trophy, and there is only One in whom I seek approval. By the power of Jesus Christ, I refuse to set my hope and dreams on a trophy that will perish. I refuse to desire the approval of men and women who serve the prince of this world. My hope is in Christ. I will press on and continue to build Champions for Jesus Christ!

A Prayer

Lord, how great you are! My Creator, Sustainer, and Redeemer! You have called me to be a Champion and to build Champions for Jesus Christ. I pray you will fill me with your Holy Spirit and empower me to stay focused on this mission. Keep my heart from the pursuits of this world and may I desire nothing this world has to offer—from the fleeting approval of man to perishable trophies.

O Lord, keep my heart with all vigilance, for from it flows the springs of life. Put away from me crooked speech, and put devious talk far from me. May my eyes look directly forward upon you, your glory, and your mission. May my gaze be straight before me as my eyes are centered upon you. Help me to bow before you and ponder the path of my feet daily, that all of my ways will be sure to honor you. O Lord, my God, my Savior, help me not to swerve to the right or to the left in the pursuits of the desires of this world—the pride of possessions, the lust of the eyes, and the lust of the flesh. Turn my feet away from evil! May I serve you wholly, Lord! May my life bring you glory and honor. Amen.

3

THE LORD BUILDS

I OFTEN SAY THERE IS no one dumber than a person who just graduated from college. I speak from experience with myself! My point is not that those kids are really dumb, but for most kids, this is the first time they will be out on their own and financially responsible for their endeavors. This will be the first time they have to work for someone who is telling them what to do and when to do it. Mom and Dad can't call in sick for them or write them a note for being late. They are totally responsible for their actions and their success. It is an eye-opening experience. They know nothing, as I knew nothing; and hopefully, they learn fast.

After college, I went into the air force and was stationed at Robins Air Force Base. My wife and I hastily got married, and our first year of marriage was a very challenging time. I was trying to make a name for myself in the air force by going in early and staying late. I have no clue what I did while I was there because newly commissioned officers don't do much (well, I didn't). But I knew to get there first and leave last. My whole life was consumed with me being successful. This does not necessarily mix well with a new marriage.

My wife and I got married, but our lives had not been surrendered to the Lord. Our whole worlds revolved around ourselves, and therefore we could not provide each other with what we needed. Instead of serving one another, I think we were both waiting to be served without serving. We were lost. We had no relationship with Jesus Christ and were not being led by him. We believed in him and but had not surrendered to him. With my new job in the air force and my prideful quest to the best in the world, our marriage hit rock bottom extremely fast.

I remember driving one Sunday night by myself, probably after an argument with my wife. The Lord was not audibly speaking to me, but it sure seemed like it. All of a sudden, my mind starts revealing things to me: "You're arrogant. You're prideful. You only care about yourself." There were a lot of other revelations about my sinful state as well. I now realize this was the Holy Spirit revealing to me my sinful nature. I knew I had to surrender my life to Jesus Christ, or the only thing I had ever committed to the Lord would end quickly in shambles—my marriage.

I went home and dropped to my knees and asked God to take all of me. Dropping to our knees is the most humbling experience in the world. But it is a sign and expression of total surrender. No one told me to drop to my knees. I guess the Holy Spirit led me to my knees. All I know is, being on my knees was the only proper way for me to surrender everything to the Lord. From that point on, my life was Christ's. Did I all of a sudden quit sinning? Of course not! Even to this day, I am a gigantic screwup. I just hope to be less and less of a screwup each year. God works on us in stages. Sanctification is growing in Jesus Christ. This is a lifelong pursuit.

A New Man in Christ

As a new man in Jesus Christ, I did understand one thing: All that I do is to be done for the glory of Jesus Christ, not for the glory of myself. I knew my marriage was important to God, and I needed his help to make it work. By the leading of the Holy Spirit, Psalm 127:1

became very important to me: "Unless the Lord builds the house, those who build it labor in vain. Unless the Lord watches over the city, the watchman stays awake in vain" (ESV).

To me, this was a very simple concept. Whatever it is that God calls us to pursue, we are to let him lead us and be our strength. We are to do it for his glory and to build his kingdom. At this particular moment, my marriage was the house. I knew I had to trust in the Lord and follow his lead. In doing this, I entrusted my marriage to him. He does not give us a magic formula and everyone's problems are different. But as we come to the Lord and ask him to build the house, trust in him, and follow his guidance, the Lord will see it through.

Listen, I'm not sitting here telling you my marriage is perfect and, I can't stand people who make those accusations. This side of heaven, nothing will ever be perfect. God continues to sanctify my wife and me, and as he does this, my wife and I grow closer and closer. I need to be a better and more loving husband. Half the time my wife is talking, I'm thinking about football. I don't even know how to fix this issue! But I love my wife more and more by the power of Christ working in me. Can I write a book on marriage? Absolutely not, as I have a whole lot of work to do. The point of me telling the story is to lay a foundation of how important it is to surrender all to the Lord and let him build the house!

My Profession as God's House

Soon after I surrendered all to the Lord, he called me into coaching football. This was extremely hard as well. I had been in the air force for three years and received my new orders to Vandenberg Air Force Base in California. Once you start your military career, you automatically fix your eyes twenty years down the road when you can retire and get 50 percent of your salary the rest of your life. In my head, I concocted the idea that I would work in the air force for twenty years and then I will coach high school football starting at forty-three. That still seems like a good plan!

However, that was my plan. I knew God had called me into coaching high school football. Through much prayer and seeking God's will, I left the air force and jumped into teaching and coaching at the high school level. It's funny looking back on it. Everyone told me I was an idiot for doing that. When you look at it on paper, they are correct. However, through prayer and spending time with God, it was clear to me that God was calling me into coaching. I could not and would not reject what God was calling me to do.

As I left the air force and jumped into coaching and teaching, I had to place total trust in the Lord to lead me. I came right back to Psalm 127:1, "Unless the Lord builds the house, those who build it labor in vain." I had to put all my trust in the Lord and follow his counsel and his lead. At this point in my life, I was consistent with Bible study and prayer with God each morning. The Holy Spirit was now using this verse to teach me about my new profession. I came to this conclusion: "God has called me into coaching, and I have no idea what I'm doing and where I'm going. I will commit everything to him. Lord, the first house I had to surrender to you was my marriage. Now I surrender to you my profession. As a coach, I need you to build me. Make me into the coach you want me to be."

In fact, I want to share to with you a card I still have in my wallet that I feel the Holy Spirit led me to write the very first year I started coaching. On the front at the top, "BE A GREAT COACH" is labeled. Then below I ask the question "How?" The answer came from Proverbs 3:5–6: "Trust in the Lord with all of your heart, and don't lean on your own understanding. In all your ways acknowledge him, and he will make straight your paths." Then at the bottom, I have written: "The Glory Goes to God," and beside this, "Every Play; Every Day."

This was the beginning of the Lord showing me to trust in him to build the house as a football coach. He had called me into coaching, and I knew I loved the game of football; but how to use it as a tool for him and build men—I had no clue. Of course, I realized later I really had no clue about coaching football either. But, praise the Lord, when he calls us to something and we trust in him, he is faithful, as we learn this in his word: "He who calls you is faithful; He will surely do it" (1 Thess. 5:24, ESV).

Life as a Head Coach for Christ

When I got the head coaching job at Eagle's Landing Christian Academy at the age of twenty-seven, I had no clue how to run a program. I didn't even have an offensive or defensive philosophy. In fact, I have no idea why they hired me. However I continued to write up on my board: "Unless the Lord builds the house, those who build labor in vain." I knew if I committed to working hard and learning, God would show me the way. I committed the program to him and asked him to lead and guide me in how to be a head football coach.

The one thing I did know how to do is work hard. I don't really have any talents, so to be any good at anything, I had to be a hard worker. My whole life, I have been a hard worker—it's all I have. I got our boys together, and we worked hard on our strength and speed. We developed a culture of hard work and commitment. This was a great foundation. We worked hard on football each day during the summer and in preseason. I came across Psalm 90:17 and started praying it consistently: "Let the favor of the Lord our God be upon us, and establish the work of our hands upon us; yes, establish the work of our hands!"

I felt like this verse fit right in with Psalm 127:1. The Lord desires to be the builder of the house and he builds through us, for we are created by God and he desires to work through us: "For we are His workmanship, created in Christ Jesus for good works, which God prepared beforehand so that we would walk in them" (Eph. 2:10, ESV). As Christ's workmanship, created to do his work and build his house, I think it is appropriate and important we pray God give us the desire to do his work and that he bless this work.

One thing we have to understand is, God teaches us through adversity. God did not teach me how to be a head coach in one day. No, I've been through many trials out on the field where God has shaped and molded me as a leader of his program. Some of my most disappointing losses have become the best sources of instruction for me. Not only have these failures helped me to become a better coach, they have helped me become a better leader for Jesus Christ. And I'm not even close to the coach and leader for Christ I want to be. However, I do know God will surely do his work in me.

You Won't Win Every Game

I have some bad news, if you think you are going to give your program or job to God and you will not have any failures. That sure would be nice but how in the world would God shape and mold us without failures? The book of James discusses the value of adversity. As we read in the Word,

> Count it all joy, my brothers, when you meet trials of various kinds, for you know that the testing of your faith produces steadfastness. And let steadfastness have its full effect, that you may be perfect and complete, lacking in nothing. (James 1:2–4 ESV)

I think you can go to any coach, and they will tell you they learn valuable lessons through losing. As Christians, one way God uses losing is to reveal to us our character. How we respond in adversity speaks volumes about who we actually are in our hearts. God is always shaping and molding our inner being so we may look more and more like him. Sometimes, losing shows us areas of pride and arrogance in our life. Oftentimes, losing helps reveal to us the treasure of our hearts.

I always pray a dangerous prayer when it comes to winning if I am looking to win every game. I don't pray for victory because I never know what God's will is. I pray that our team does its absolute best and we execute flawlessly. I then pray that the Lord gives us exactly what we need in order to become more like him. My number 1 desire for our program is, we all become more and more like Christ. Even though I'd rather just beg God for a victory and have him give it to me, I know growth in Jesus Christ oftentimes requires adversity. I know God will give me the strength to handle adversity when it comes.

As I write this, we just lost our last game in the semifinals. We had an excellent team that returned a strong core of players from the previous year's state championship team. Once the season got started, we turned out to be a very dominant team. Our quarterback, who I believe was one of the best high school football players in the state of Georgia, was our leader. He could run and pass, which made defending him a nightmare. As we entered into the state playoffs, we were dominating everyone. Midway through the third quarter of the first-round playoff game, he broke his leg.

I know in his life and in our football team's life, we were left to ask *why*. We were rolling right along, and we were headed toward another state championship. Even with our QB out, our team continued to play well, but we lost in overtime of the semifinal game. We were once again left the question *why*.

It Is the Purpose of the Lord That Will Stand

Of course, we are often left with the question *why*. I take comfort in scripture, as I trust God's sovereign hand in my life: "Many are the plans in the mind of man, but it is the purpose of the Lord that will stand" (Prov. 19:21). God is sovereign and his purposes and plans will also stand. It is completely my responsibility to plan and prepare, to the best of my ability. This is the part that God has given me control over. However, the outcome and the end result is the purpose of the Lord.

As I have surrendered all to the Lord, I am at peace with the outcome of events in my life. I trust and depend upon Christ completely. It is only when we get our eyes off Jesus Christ and being a Champion for him, we become angry at what he has ordained in our lives. I truly believe God will always grant us peace and keep us free from anger as we keep our eyes on him.

This does not mean we will not, at times, be disappointed and disheartened at certain events in our life. I don't know why God had our quarterback break his leg. God's sees the whole picture, and I do not. As I lay down my life at the feet of the Creator and Savior of this world, I completely trust his will in all things. Maybe it was time for a young tenth grader to emerge and prove he was ready. I do not know. I do know that God always has his will and my best interest working together. The purpose of the Lord is good, and it will stand!

Be Strong and Courageous

We can never cower in this world about our dependence and trust in Christ. The world will try and mock us and tell us we are foolish. We live in the same world that crucified Jesus Christ. As followers of him we will surely not receive everyone's approval. We must stand strong and courageous in Jesus Christ. As we work to build his Kingdom it is He who will go before us, go with us and clean up after us as we work.

I do not know exactly what God has called you to do. No matter your occupation or your position in life, we are to be living testimonies for Jesus Christ. We must live bold and courageously for Jesus Christ. I love the command that God gave Joshua as he handed the reigns over to him after Moses died:

> Have I not commanded you? Be strong and courageous. Do not be frightened, and do not be dismayed, for the LORD your God is with you wherever you go. (Josh.1:9, ESV)

We serve and worship an awesome and omnipotent God. As we surrender all to Christ and allow the Holy Spirit to fully abide in us, God will empower us with this strong and courageous spirit. God commands us to be faithful. As we trust the Lord to build the house, fear and dismay should never enter our hearts. Even though we may see failure everywhere we look, we have a God working through us who knows no obstacle. God wants our full trust and surrender in him. Where will our strength and courage come? Jesus Christ.

To sum up being strong and courageous in Christ, I refer to the following scripture King David wrote to God:

> Nevertheless, I am continually with you; you hold my right hand. You guide me with your counsel, and afterward you will receive me to glory. Who have I in heaven but you? And there is nothing on earth that I desire besides you. My flesh and my heart may fail, but God is the strength of my heart and my portion forever (Ps. 73:23–26, ESV).

Victory Belongs to the Lord

As you are building for the Lord, be very careful you do not get prideful and arrogant when you have success. I love Proverbs 21:31: "The horse is made ready for battle, but victory belongs to the Lord." St. Augustine, the great theologian from the fourth and fifth century, is quoted as saying, "Pray as if everything depends upon God; work as if everything depends upon you." God is sovereign and in control of all things. We are to work with all diligence, for this is the responsibility he gave to us. But when comes success, it is from the Lord.

Anytime we have success here on this earth, we must rejoice in the Lord. If I am good at anything, it is because the Lord has given me the ability. Food on our table is a victory from the Lord. All that we have and all that we are is from the Lord. The joy is in the work; the glory is in Jesus Christ! All that I am, all that I have—my heart beating, my brain thinking, the water I drink, the food I eat—all of it is from the Lord.

Bless the Lord, Oh My Soul

As I think about what great things the Lord has done—first and foremost, him dying on the cross and shedding his blood so that we might have forgiveness from our sins—my heart rejoices in Christ. We live in a world that wants God to bless them with material blessings and worldly victories. People travel in thousands to listen to ministers preach a gospel that revolves around how God can bless you with these worldly things. Have we ever stopped to think that it is our job to bless the Lord?

We serve a God who came to die for us. He saved us from the wrath of God, provided us with victory over sin, and we now have access to God through the blood of Jesus Christ. What a blessing. We are now, in turn, to be living sacrifices for the Jesus Christ. We are to bear his image and be reflections of his glory in this world. We are to walk with him and abide in him. We are to build his house.

A Prayer

O Lord, how great you are, my God and my King! By the blood of Jesus Christ, I have forgiveness from my sins and everlasting life! O Lord, in all my endeavors and accomplishments, even in my worldly failures, may I bless the Lord. Oh my soul and all that is within me, may I bless your Holy Name! May I never try and build my own house for my own glory. Lord, I have been made to bring you glory and honor. May I trust in you wholly. I do pray you grant me success in all my endeavors. I pray that all my endeavors glorify you. May I always seek your call and your will, for then you will guide me. May everything I put my mind and my hand to, may it be you who works in me to build. How great you are, my Hope and my Trust. To you, O Lord, all the honor and the glory and the praise. Amen.

4

UNDIVIDED DEDICATION

UNDIVIDED DEDICATION IS UNINTERRUPTED INTENSITY on the mission or goal. *Intensity* can be defined "as focused effort." It is easy to see how undivided dedication can be used as a coach. We want our players focused on the pursuit of winning, and we want nothing to get in the way. We desire they come to practice and forget about their relationship problems or problems they are having at home. We like to think our practices are a place of refuge, a place a player can come and escape life for a few hours. This certainly benefits us. We demand undivided dedication to the cause of winning. No distractions are allowed. Give us your all!

Obviously, as a coach, I demand undivided dedication from my players. However, as I demand this from them I need to be undividedly dedicated to them.

If a player only has value to me for what he or she can do as an athlete, then my dedication to that player is divided. When we only care for them when they can help us win, we are not dedicated to them. As coaches, we need to quit asking players to do things for us that we do not do for them. If we are going to ask them to have undivided dedication for us in the sport we coach, we need to first model being undividedly dedicated in their lives. The only way we can do this is through love. I'm not talking about the soft type of love portrayed in our world. I am talking about love the way God intended it to be—committed, unwavering, passionate, and resilient.

What Love Is Not

Before we venture into discussing love, let's discuss what love is *not*. The way our world knows love, love is self-serving. We love people when they have something to offer us. People are blind to this fact, but it is true. We will love someone as long as they love us and have something we desire. We will love our players as long as they work hard and produce on the field so we can win games. We will love our bosses as long as they give us what we want. We will love our wives as long as we continue to desire them and they serve us. There is no doubt you will become a champion when you love this way. The key word is *you* will become a champion. You will have done nothing to help build Champions around you. How often do we see leaders who are great but their family is in shambles? They are champions in their profession, but everything that is important to God is their failure.

Bottom line—the world's love is really selfishness. We hear about men or women all the time telling their spouses, "I just don't love you anymore." I can just see that coach who tells his wife he doesn't love her anymore and then he will go and tell his team, "There is no *I* in *team*." Probably the softest term in the world to me is the worldly version of the word *love*. It is a self-serving, fleeting emotion.

Make no mistake: you can win with this version of love. You can be the best coach, teacher, CEO, or whatever; but you will not be investing in the lives of your people for the kingdom of God. As a coach, with this worldly version of love, I will be great at developing my players in the game they love and they may become the best in their profession, but they will be losers in the areas God cares about. However, remember, as Christian coaches, we are not after creating the best players in the world—if that happens, praise God—we are interested in building Champions for Jesus Christ.

Christ Is the Example of Love

The word *love* is a very powerful word if defined properly. *Love* is sacrificial resolve to stay faithful and committed to a cause greater than self. Undivided dedication describes love. Jesus sums it up for us with his definition: "Greater love has no one than this, that someone lay down his life for his friends" (John 15:13, ESV). This is the language of dying to self. Love is putting my desires, my needs, and my wants aside and wholeheartedly serving another.

As Christians, we are called to be imitators of God. God is love. He sent his son Jesus Christ to die for our sins as the greatest the example of love: "Therefore be imitators of God, as beloved children. And walk in love, as Christ loved us and gave himself up for us, a fragrant offering and sacrifice to God" (Eph. 5:1–2, ESV). In our culture, love tells us to go with our hearts and to make ourselves happy. This is the exact opposite of Christ's example. Love was not just a feeling—rather, a sacrifice. He counted others as more significant, and he looked to their interests. He did not want to be butchered and then slaughtered on a cross. However, he endured and paid the penalty for our sin so we would not have to. This is sacrifice. Sacrifice is love.

The reason the world does not want to hear this true definition of love is because this type of love requires discipline. The words *commitment, faithfulness,* and *sacrifice* are required for this type of love; these are not easy words. When I use those words, I am dying to my desires and wants for the service of another. This is the hardest thing for any man or woman in the world to do. We can only have the love that Christ describes through the power of the Holy Spirit. If we can learn to love like Christ, we will become very powerful people in building his kingdom.

The words *commitment, faithfulness,* and *sacrifice* are not hard words when they can get me something. If I work hard as a coach and commit to doing my best, we may win some games. If I stay faithful to my diet, I may lose some weight. If I sacrifice a little extra time and study more, maybe I will get smarter. They aren't easy things to do, but they are not intimidating. If I fail, I only let myself down. I can handle that.

Our culture has taught us to make these words about us. "I will stay faithful and committed to my wife, as long I still love her"—see, the hard words *faithful* and *committed* are still revolving around *my* feelings. Our feelings are whimsical and change like the direction of the wind. If we are going to live our life according to our feelings, we will let everyone down around us. If we are going to love according to our feelings, then *love* is the weakest word in the human language.

Contrary to how *love* is seemingly defined in our culture, it is the most powerful word in the Gospel. God is love. The greatest example of love he gave us was sending his son Jesus Christ to die on the cross for our sins. Jesus Christ's humble submission was an example of love. In both cases, the subject was not the recipient of love. Love is an action we do to other people. Love involves other people, and this is where it gets challenging.

Love is commitment, faithfulness, and sacrifice to the desires and needs of another. It isn't putting our desires second either; it is being nonexistent to our desires. Love is dying to what we want and what we desire and serving others. Love is unwavering commitment to something else besides me. Love is sacrificing my desires for the greater good of another!

Love Your Players

When I stand before a group of young men, I am standing before a group of young men made in the image of God. God tells us each of us is his creation and we are fearfully and wonderfully made:

> I praise you, for I am fearfully and wonderfully made. Wonderful are your works; my soul knows it very well. My frame was not hidden from you, when I was being made in secret, intricately woven in the depths of the earth. Your eyes saw my unformed substance; in your book were written, every one of them, the days that were formed for me, when as yet there was none of them. (Ps. 139:14–16, ESV)

As a coach, this is intimidating. Every single player I stand before God has been made in God's image and for his glory with the loving care. He loved each one of them so much that he sacrificed his Son. I love my son more than anything; and it is convicting to know that God loves my players, my son, and me more than I love my son. We are coaching God's children, and that is a daunting responsibility we should not take lightly.

Therefore, I must coach these boys with love. There is no other way to define the way God expects me to coach. I must pray earnestly that God teach me how to love my players. I must be committed to them, faithful to them, and sacrifice for them for the kingdom of God. If I do not love them, nothing I do will have an impact on them for their life on this earth and the one to come. Loving my players with the love of Jesus Christ must drive all that I do. *Wow*, this is something only the Holy Spirit can do through me. I need his power and strength in me at all times.

Undivided Dedication

As I learn to love my players with the love of Jesus Christ, I become undivided in my dedication to building Champions for Jesus Christ. There is no alternate motive for coaching my players. I am not using them for personal gain. I look at each player as a child of God, and I desperately want to invest in his life for the kingdom of God. As a football coach, I hope I am laying seeds that will help my young men grow up to be faithful husbands, loving fathers, and men who will impact their community for Jesus Christ. By the power of the Holy Spirit that works in me, I am undivided in my dedication to the mission God has given me—to build Champions for Jesus Christ.

King David Had Undivided Dedication

Christians get a bad rap in the world, and we are often labeled physically and mentally weak. I guess since a Christian admits defeat in sin and the need of a Savior, this looks weak and helpless in the eyes of the world. This really makes no sense. Christians are the ones who have the answer to sins curse on man, which is death. This is Jesus Christ. Furthermore, I argue Christians are not physically or mentally weak, and I think King David is one of our greatest examples.

We can learn a great deal from King David. From the first time we are introduced to King David in the Bible, it is apparent he has a heart to serve God. He earnestly sought to please God. He trusted in God as his source of power and strength as he understood God is our Creator and Sustainer. Yes, I do realize David failed in many areas, but he suffered the ramifications of his sin. In all his mistakes, he always repented and turned back to God. We must do the same!

King David, the mighty warrior, put all his hope and trust in God. He was a mighty man of God, and the Bible tells us that David killed tens of thousands in battle. We also can read about him killing lions and bears. In fact, I believe King David was a warrior unparalleled by any warrior we would know today. The closest thing we see is a Navy SEAL or a member of Delta Force. Don't get me wrong; I think these men are the toughest in the world. However, King David killed people with a sword and slingshot. He didn't have the modern-day technology we see today. It is obvious the Lord blessed him with unparalleled power and strength in order to accomplish his purposes. King David understood this power came from the Lord.

Even though King David had his faults, he was undivided in his dedication to the Lord. He knew the Lord was his source of power and strength. He wholeheartedly sought to accomplish the Lord's purpose in his life. Even though God granted him unparalleled power and strength, King David never sought to use this to get honor and glory for himself. He was always diligent to seek the Lord and serve the Lord. He knew his salvation was in Jesus Christ. King David, one of the strongest and fiercest warriors, is the author of these words:

> Blessed be the LORD, my rock,
> who trains my hands for war,
> and my fingers for battle;
> he is my steadfast love and my fortress,
> my stronghold and my deliverer,
> my shield and he in whom I take refuge,
> who subdues peoples under me. (Ps. 144:1–2, ESV)

As a Christian who loves to compete and to win, I love to know of men like King David who were warriors yet put their hope and trust in Christ. King David acknowledges that God controls all things, even down to his hands and fingers for battle. The world calls Christians weak, but there are countless examples of some very powerful men in the Bible who accredited all that they were to Christ.

What we need to glean from King David is that he sought God. He desired to know God and he pursued him:

> O God, you are my God; earnestly I seek you;
> my soul thirsts for you;
> my flesh faints for you,
> as in a dry and weary land where there is no
> water. (Ps. 63:1, ESV)

I find these words beautiful. Here is this mighty warrior who can kill thousands in battle, and he is humbling himself before the Lord. We can be mighty warriors and surrender all to Jesus Christ. We can be men who are the fiercest competitors and love to win and, yet still, surrender all to God. Being a Christian does not make us weak; it makes us stronger! May we be undivided in our dedication to Jesus Christ; for in this is power!

A Prayer

> O Lord, how great you are, my King and my Redeemer! You are my Trust and my Hope. Lord, I pray you would teach me what love truly means and then lead me in my pursuit to love the way Jesus Christ loved us.
>
> First and foremost, help me to love my wife and my son. May I not be swayed by my fleeting emotions, but may I be rooted in love. This love of Christ produces unwavering commitment, dying to self, and service to others. These words describe undivided dedication.
>
> Lord, help me to love my players and the coaches with whom you have placed me. May I never look at them as men who are there to

help me win and be successful, but may I have undivided dedication as I seek to help them become Champions for Jesus Christ. Lord, teach me your ways; teach me to love like Christ. Lord, help me to be patient and kind; help me to not be envious and never boastful; help me to not be arrogant or rude. Help me to not insist on my own way; help me to not be irritable or resentful; help me to not rejoice in wrongdoing, but help me to rejoice with the truth.

Help me to bear all things, believe all things, hope in all things, and endure all things. Amen.

5

WHOLLY FOR CHRIST

NOPE, I DIDN'T NOT MISSPELL *wholly. Wholly for Christ* means "all of me." Not part of me, not 99 percent of me, but all of me dedicated to doing the will of the Lord. I exist to serve Jesus Christ and build his kingdom. I have been made in his image and for his glory. I once was enslaved to sin, but now I have been set loose by the blood of Jesus Christ. I once looked at death and had no answer, but now death has been defeated through Christ. I have eternal life in Christ. Therefore, because of the love, commitment, and sacrifice Christ has shown me, I will wholly serve him. Not my will Lord, but yours!

I have defined *love* as sacrificial resolve to stay faithful and committed to a cause greater than self. It requires giving all of myself. We discussed how undivided dedication is a description of love. Before we can ever love another person, we must give our full commitment and allegiance to Christ. All of me, all that I am, and all that I do belong to Christ. I must be unwavering in my commitment to him. I must have undivided dedication in pursuing him. I must be wholly his. I must hold nothing back for myself. I must seek him in all that I do. As I do give myself wholly to Christ, he comes in and fills me with his strength and power through his Holy Spirit and empowers me to love like Christ.

Wholly for Christ is 100 percent commitment to Christ. The commitment God has should give us an understanding of commitment. We don't do something if we are not wholly committed. Once we decide we are going to do something, we jump in and give all that we have. The Bible gives some examples of men who were not wholly committed:

> If any of you lacks wisdom, let him ask God, who gives generously to all without reproach, and it will be given him. But let him ask in faith, with no doubting, for the one who doubts is like a wave of the sea that is driven and tossed by the wind. For that person must not suppose that he will receive anything from the Lord; he is a double-minded man, unstable in all his ways. (James 1:5–8, ESV)

When we come to Christ and give him all of ourselves, we are entrusting our life to him. We trust in Christ and his plan for our life. We go forward in our endeavors with conviction and confidence. However, the double-minded man is a man who doubts and is unsure of himself. He can't make a decision because he has no confidence in his commitments and convictions. He is tossed back and forth by the opinions of man. He is consumed with his desire to please the world and man. He has the desire to only serve himself. He is full of worldly love, which is self-serving and only exists as long as his needs and desires are being fulfilled. This man has an appearance of strength on the surface but is weak at the core.

The man who is wholly devoted to Christ has power from Christ. He seeks to please the Lord and this provides singleness of purpose. His gaze is directly forward and on Jesus Christ. He knows the one in whom he serves and seeks solely to please the King of this universe, the one who holds this universe together by his mere breath. The man who is wholly devoted to Christ is not tossed back and forth by the ideas and thoughts of the world. Being *wholly devoted to Christ* results in unwavering strength!

Total Surrender

How does a man wholly commit to anything? Total surrender. This is where we must begin if we are going to be effective for God's kingdom. I believe God has made me a football coach as a means to build godly men. As a coach, for God to be able to use me, I must first surrender. There is power in surrender. If I am going to lead for Jesus Christ, I must first surrender all to him. If he is going to be able to work through me and impact the young men I coach every day, I must sacrifice my life to Christ. As I die to myself, surrendering all to Christ, he will come in and live through me. This is how totally surrendering all that I am to Christ becomes total strength.

As a leader of young men, I want them to surrender all of themselves to the greater good of the team. I want them to die to their selfish desires and their selfish agenda and seek to play for their brothers on the field. There is power in surrendering all to the team. When eleven men step onto the field looking to do what is best for the team and playing hard for their teammates, great things will happen. A team is a reflection of its leadership.

Total surrender begins with the head coach and the coaching staff. I believe there is nothing more powerful than the players seeing their coach's surrender to a cause greater than themselves. Many of them will not accept Christ while we are coaching them, but they are seeing a life surrendered to Christ modeled to them daily. This is a powerful tool God will use in their future.

As a coach, total surrender is the boys sacrificing their personal desires and serving their teammates. As coaches, we often talk about the magic of chemistry. Teams that have good chemistry are selfless teams. When there is no selfish agenda and boys are playing for a common goal, the team has a chance to be magical. This same mentality must be carried over to our walk with Christ. We must surrender all our desires at the feet of Christ and seek him with undivided dedication. Not my will, Lord, but yours! Now, God can use us, and we can be effective for his kingdom.

A Man Who Did Not Surrender

The Bible is full of examples for us to learn from. Growing up, I was always intrigued by Samson whose life is chronicled in Judges 13–16. I wanted to be Samson because of the amazing strength God gave him. I was like most young boys—I wanted to be strong and be a warrior. From conception, the Lord had a specific call on Samson's life to save the Israelites from the Philistines. Samson was to be devoted to God, and God would use him to free the Israelites from Philistine enslavement.

As a young man, two verses drew me to Samson. An angel of the Lord approached Samson's mother after she conceived him and describes the powerful call on Samson's life: "He shall begin to save Israel from the hand of the Philistines" (Judg. 13:5, ESV). Who doesn't want to conquer an enemy and lead a group of people into freedom? I grew up on He-Man. I wanted to be that guy. Samson was called from the beginning to be an actual He-Man for God.

After Samson grew up, he had to turn himself over to the Philistines. When I was younger, I kind of glossed over the fact that his sin led him to turn himself over to the Philistines. I didn't really understand this, I didn't see it, but I could envision what he did when he turned himself over. The Philistines led him into their territory to turn him over to the ruling officials. They had bound Samson in ropes and marched him to their city. Samson could not handle it and power from God rushed upon him:

When he came to Lehi, the Philistines came shouting to meet him. Then the Spirit of the LORD rushed upon him, and the ropes that were on his arms became as flax that has caught fire, and his bonds melted off his hands. And he found a fresh jawbone of a donkey, and put out his hand and took it, and with it he struck 1,000 men. (Judg. 15:14–15, ESV)

Wow! What a powerful man. He snaps the ropes that bind his hands together and goes and finds and jawbone of a donkey. Once he snapped the ropes that bound him, I am sure he was looking for anything that he can use to destroy his enemy. The closest thing to him was the jawbone of a donkey. Samson was so powerful that he used this as a weapon and killed a thousand men. He didn't use a machine gun and just hose people down. He used a bone—amazing! I always knew *Rambo, Braveheart,* and *Gladiator* were just movies. Even though I wanted to be each of those men, I knew it was all a little fabricated. But Samson is not fabricated. The Bible is the inerrant Word of God. Samson was a mighty warrior. I actually wished my parents named me Samson!

I now understand Samson made decisions that did not please the Lord and his life ended in his own demise due to the poor decisions he made over and over. The story of Samson serves as a warning to me. It is a great example of what will happen if we do not wholly surrender our lives to the Lord.

The Lord's promise is that He would use Samson to deliver the Israelites from the hand of the Philistines. The power that resided in Samson was from the Lord. The Bible is clear to identify his strength was from the Lord. However, Samson lived a life that did not acknowledge this. Samson constantly did what he wanted to do without inquiry or fear of the Lord. He was extremely selfish and lived life entirely in the flesh. In fact, now, when I read the story of Samson, I am praying that God protect me from the mistakes of Samson.

It is quickly evident in scripture Samson's problem: he always did what is right in his own eyes. God warned the Israelites from marrying Philistine women. These women worshiped and served foreign gods, and this would be a detriment to Israelite men. The pursuit of these women would lead to the men rejecting the Lord and serving foreign gods. Samson knew God's rule but had total disregard for it because he was not seeking to bring glory to God with his life or his actions. He only cared to do what was right in his own eyes and please his flesh. He tells his parents about the first Philistine woman whom he desired but God had warned against: "Get her for me, for she is right in my eyes" (Judg. 14:3, ESV).

The Book of Judges quickly describes the horrible outcome for Samson after he married her. Then we see his total demise as a leader as he falls in love with another Philistine woman, Delilah. We read about Samson making the same mistake he made the first time. Samson was so blind in his sin, he could not learn from previous mistakes. He falls in love with Delilah, and the Philistines use Delilah to lay a trap for and to capture Samson. Samson goes off to jail where they gouged out his eyes and left him blind. There was now little hope for Israel. The one in whom God had raised up and given power to defeat the Philistines was now blind, powerless, and in jail.

As we focus on Samson's ability to lead for Christ, we see that he was completely inept. I believe God's desire was for him to not only lead the Israelites in their conquest against the enslavement of the Philistines but also lead the Israelites to the Lord. Samson completely missed this call on his life. Even though he rebelled against God's commands, the Lord still used him to accomplish his purposes.

God's purpose will not be thwarted, and he will use us all for his kingdom. He uses some while we are completely surrendered to him, and he uses other in their rebellion. Satan's rebellion was not a shock to God and did not thwart his plan. Pontius Pilate handing Jesus over to be crucified did not alter God's plan. God is sovereign and omniscient; his plans and his ways always prevail. I think he allows us to humbly submit to him and play an active role in his plans or to reject his ways like Samson.

Samson's life is an example of a man who did not surrender. It ended in his death, with God still killing three thousand philistines. I believe if Samson had surrendered all to God and followed him, his life would not have ended the way it did. It is a warning to me to serve God and follow his commands. God will accomplish his purposes through us. I pray my heart wholly obeys him. By rejecting God, Samson did not influence God's people the way he could have. He never fully reached his purpose in Christ because he did not live for Christ. In spite of this, God still used him.

Now, the big question I always think about is, since God still used Samson, did he go to heaven? The Bible is clear that if we are living a life refusing to obey God, we are not true followers of God:

> On that day many will say to me, 'Lord, Lord, did we not prophesy in your name, and cast out demons in your name, and do many mighty works in your name?' And then will I declare to them, 'I never knew you; depart from me, you workers of lawlessness.' (Matt. 7:22–23, ESV)

Once Samson fell prey to Delilah's deception and was put in prison, he remained there for the rest of his life. I think he had an opportunity to reflect back on the foolishness of his actions, how he rejected serving and living for God. I think he repented and became a man wholly for Christ. The reason I think this is because he was looking for a chance to serve the Lord at the end of his life. God gave him another opportunity, and he broke the pillars that held a building of three thousand Philistine men and women who were worshiping their worthless god. Unfortunately, Samson died as well. God promises to forgive us of our sins, but we are left with the ramifications of our sin.

Having the Appearance of Godliness but Denying Its Power

When I read about Samson, I am reminded of Paul's warning to Timothy. Paul is warning Timothy of the ungodliness he will see in the last days. This ungodliness is primarily from those who profess to know Christ yet do not live in Christ and, therefore, lack the power to live a life that glorifies Christ:

> For people will be lovers of self, lovers of money, proud, arrogant, abusive, disobedient to their parents, ungrateful, unholy, heartless, unappeasable, slanderous, without self-control, brutal, not loving good, treacherous, reckless, swollen with conceit, lovers of pleasure rather than lovers of God, having the appearance of godliness, but denying its power. Avoid such people. (2 Tim. 3:2–5, ESV)

Not only should we avoid such people, we must guard against becoming like these people. I do not want to be a man who claims Christ but lives a life that is completely in rebellion against him. Before I surrendered all to Christ, I was this man. Apart from the power of Christ working in me, I am still this man. Before I devoted my life wholly to Christ through complete surrender, I used to argue the existence of God and the purpose of Jesus Christ to everyone who came across my path; but I had no power in Christ. I ran to sin. Even though I knew certain things were wrong, I was enslaved to sin's power over me. This lifestyle leads to one just accepting sin as a part of their lifestyle. See, there was a form of godliness in me in that I would proclaim the name of Jesus Christ. The problem was there was no power. I had not surrendered my life to Christ. Just like Samson, apart from a life surrendered to Christ, we will be ruled by sin.

Operation G220

Once we have surrendered all to the Lord, our life in Christ is a process, and God continues to sanctify us each and every day. As God continues to refine me, Galatians 2:20 is a powerful verse God has used to impact my steps:

> I have been crucified with Christ. It is no longer I who live, but Christ who lives in me. And the life I now live in the flesh I live by faith in the Son of God, who loved me and gave himself for me. (Gal. 2:20, ESV)

The apostle Paul does not leave any confusion in his language, does he? As Christians, we are to die to our sinful desires, be crucified with Christ, and we are to now live in Christ. This is language of total surrender. This is the language of whole commitment. No man can be wholly committed until he surrenders to the cause. No man can surrender all to Christ until he humbles himself. Probably the hardest words for man are, "Not my will, O God, but your will." Only the broken, humble man who has surrendered all can say those words. Although these are the hardest words to say, they are a source of power that is uncommon to the common man.

There is a difference between believing and surrendering, as said in the Bible: "Even the demons believe—and shudder" (James 2:19, ESV). Samson believed. Coaches know the difference between believing and surrendering as well. It's the difference between having a group of young men and women that are showing up to practice and trying to get through the day compared to a group who comes to practice and gives everything they have because they want to win. The first group I could care less to coach. However, the group that has surrendered to be the best they can be, this is the group that has a chance to do great things.

I believe God views it the same way. If not, Jesus would not have stated, "Not everyone who says to me, 'Lord, Lord,' will enter the kingdom of heaven, but the one who does the will of my Father who is in heaven" (Matt. 7:21). Yes this is hard teaching, but as coaches we demand the same thing—you are either wholly bought in or you are a fence-sitter. We don't want any fence-sitters! We don't want players who are tossed to and fro by the wind. We want players who are wholly committed to the cause and wholly bought in to the coaching staff! As coaches, we are finite creatures and we demand undivided dedication to the cause. How much more so does God—the Infinite Creator of all things—demand undivided dedication? May we strive to give God our all!

A Prayer

O Lord, my God and my King, I am a finite creature, and my knowledge is limited. But you, O Lord, are Sovereign: you know all things and control all things. You, O Lord, are omnipotent: you are all powerful. You, O Lord, are omniscient: you know all things. Man is a fool not to seek you and live for you. Lord, in our sinful state, we do not seek you and we do not live for you. We are self-worshipers and only seek the good of ourselves. We use people to get what we want and disguise it as love. We are only committed to causes that will bring us glory and honor. We love those who love us and serve us. We hate and do not care for those who have no value in our pursuit of personal glory and fame. O Lord, I hate this person that dwells within me. Daily I come to you, begging that this sinful man be crucified with Christ. May it no longer by I who live but Christ who lives in me. Help me, Lord, that the life I now live in the flesh I may live by faith in the Son of God, who loves me and gave himself for me. How great you are, my God and King. May I be wholly committed to you! Amen.

6

TAKE OWNERSHIP

I SEE TWO COMMON CHARACTERISTICS in people: (1) we like to sit around and wait for someone else to step up and lead and (2) we like to blame others when we fail. I hear people blaming the president or the preacher for their problems all the time. On a smaller scale, they may blame the leader of the school, business, or community. I often wonder what our world would be like if people took responsibility for everything that happened to them. What if people led instead of complained? What if people took ownership of the problem instead of blaming someone?

Kids come into the weight room complaining about how hard certain teachers are and making excuses for their bad grades. Oftentimes, they are visibly upset. I tell them that being upset does nothing for them. No one cares if they are upset, and in fact, I find it quite funny. I want them to understand that being upset is a waste of energy. Furthermore, they are upset with their teacher in making a poor grade when, in reality, it is their fault they made a poor grade. They didn't study; they didn't pay attention in class each day; they didn't take their homework seriously.

Blaming the teacher doesn't do any good. The teacher isn't going to change. If he or she is hard, they aren't going to become easy. The kid can't sit around and wait for the teacher to change if he wants a good grade. He is going to have to take ownership of his actions and start working harder. The young man comes in complaining, feeling as if he has no power over his grade. He feels hopeless. This is crazy because he has all the power. He feels like he is a victim of his circumstances, but in reality, he must take ownership of his circumstances.

Taking ownership is taking responsibility by removing all distractions and obstacles that impair one from reaching his or her goal. For this young man we are discussing, I tell him he needs to study two hours a night, sit in the front row of the class, do his homework thoroughly, and then meet with his teacher twice a week, requesting an update on his progress. Yes, he is going to have to not watch TV, turn his computer off, and turn his phone off. These things are usually why kids are failing class. He is going to have to discipline himself to sitting down and making his mind focus. He may or may not be willing to do these things, but if he wants a good grade, he is going to have to take ownership of his actions.

These things are extremely hard for kids to do; they are extremely hard for adults to do. We want to text all day, play on the internet and social media, and run around with our friends all night—this is goofing off. If we don't rule our actions, our actions will rule us. We always want to do what is fun and enjoyable, and we run to do those things. And those things are good in moderation. However, if we are going to have success, we have to discipline ourselves to doing those things we don't want to do. I like to say, "The things we hate are the things that will make us great." We must embrace the hard things in life and work hard to be our best at them. We must take ownership of our actions.

So, to the young man who can't do well in class: Take Ownership. Sit your tail down and study. Focus on your teacher in class and everything they have to say. Take every single note you possible take. Go home and rewrite them and memorize them. Throw your TV, phone, and internet provider in the trash. Oh, the pain of discipline! Quit blaming your teacher, young man, and Take Ownership! Demand excellence from yourself!

Taking Ownership of Leading for Christ

There are two approaches to leadership we can consider as Christians: (1) *godly leadership*, which is motivating a group of men and women by asking them to die to their selfish desires and their flesh to accomplish a mission that will bring glory to Jesus Christ; and (2) *worldly leadership*—motivating a group of men and women by appealing to their selfish desires and their flesh to accomplish a mission that will bring more glory to their name and ours.

Once I had defined the mission and understood the importance of the calling God has granted me as a Christian coach, I must continually take ownership of the process toward godly leadership. Leading for Jesus Christ is my responsibility. As the head coach of my football team, I understand that everyone is watching me (especially when we lose), and it is imperative that I lead for Jesus Christ. It is not an assignment I am willing to give to someone else. I will take ownership of the calling.

There is a great quote that our athletic director loves to say, which states, "Your actions speak so much louder than your words." Of course, we use this with kids when they are saying they are giving great effort and they aren't. Or they may be telling us that something is important to them but what they are showing us is completely different. Their actions are not matching their talking. As a coach, I encounter this all the time.

The apostle Paul understood the importance of his actions proving his talk. He knew people would watch him and analyze. He was so confident in his leadership for Christ that he could boldly proclaim, "Imitate me, as I imitate Christ" (1 Cor. 11:1, ESV). The New International Version of the Bible gives a better interpretation for leaders to understand: "Follow my example, as I follow the example of Christ." Now that is leadership. Follow me, do what I do, and I will lead the way. I want to be able to say this to my players, parents, coaches, fans, administrators, and teachers.

Do Not Assign Spiritual Leadership to Someone Else

As a coach who desires to make an impact in the lives of my players for Jesus Christ, I cannot pawn off spiritual leadership. I must be the leader. I can't expect the FCA guy or the chaplain to be the only leaders spiritually. These men are tools I can use for further accountability, but they can't be the leader. The leaders must lead! The coaching staff must lead. All my players' eyes are on me because I am the head coach. On our team, we do have a chaplain; but we don't have to, in order for the kids to see Christ. I will lead for Christ by the power of Christ working in me. I desire to live by Paul's creed: "Imitate me, as I imitate Christ." I pray God empowers us with the desire and the ability to lead our team with our actions.

Now, you may not be the head coach or the ultimate leader. Everyone must take ownership in leading for Christ. If you call yourself a Christian, people will be watching you. They are waiting for you to fail and to mess up so they can label all Christians hypocrites. I challenge you to take to heart what Paul tells the Corinthians: "Be on your guard; stand firm in the faith; be courageous; be strong" (1 Cor. 16:13, NIV).

God has called any man who is standing before men and women as a leader to an incredible kingdom-changing opportunity. I truly believe coaches are God's frontline warriors. We also can be the devil's biggest assets as well. We must understand that just because our FCA guy is leading for Christ, this does not mean the coach is leading for Christ. Through his actions, the coaches are either going to reinforce or make a mockery of what the FCA guy is teaching. God has given coaches a tremendous responsibility to lead through our actions and words. We are the leaders! I challenge us all: Can we all say—like Paul—to our players, coaches, parents, fans, administrators, and teachers, "Imitate me, as I imitate Christ"?

The Lord Is My Strength

The All-Powerful God of the universe, who has created the heavens and the earth, who has knitted me together in my mother's womb, who knew of my existence long ago—He is my source of strength. King David, one of the mightiest warriors and kings who ever existed in the history of man, wrote Psalm 18, and it is so powerful:

> I love you, O Lord, my strength.
> The Lord is my rock and my fortress and
>   my deliverer,
> my God, my rock, in whom I take refuge,
> my shield, and the horn of my salvation, my
>   stronghold.
> I call upon the Lord, who is worthy to
>   be praised,
> and I am saved from my enemies. (Ps.
>   18:1–3, ESV)

How in the world can I have an impact on our players for Jesus Christ? By abiding in Christ and letting him work through me.
   Later on in the same psalm, David proclaims,

> For who is God, but the Lord?
> And who is a rock, except our God?—
> the God who equipped me with strength
> and made my way blameless.
> He made my feet like the feet of a deer

and set me secure on the heights.
He trains my hands for war,
so that my arms can bend a bow of bronze.
    (Ps. 18:31–34, ESV)

God gives us the power to be great leaders for his kingdom. Just as he equipped David with strength, feet like a deer, and trained his hands for war, He will also prepare us to be effective leaders for his kingdom. As we seek the Lord and call out to him, he will lead us and teach us the way in which we should go. I am not telling you that he is going to give each of us great worldly success each year, but I do know he will lead us and empower us to lead boldly for his kingdom. We must seek him. We must trust him.

Take Ownership and Let God Direct Your Steps

Along with Galatians 2:20, Proverbs 3:5–6 is a verse I think about daily:

Trust in the Lord with all your heart, and do
not lean on your own understanding. In all
your ways acknowledge him, and he will make
straight your paths. (ESV)

If we are going to lead for Jesus Christ, we must let him lead the way. We must die to our selfish agenda and follow Christ. This verse clearly identifies that we should not lean on our own understanding but trust in the Lord. We must take ownership as we let God direct our steps. We must spend time seeking God daily and allow the Holy Spirit to lead us.

Can you imagine a football team if they went to practice for two and a half hours each day and no coach was with them and were left to themselves and expected to figure things out? This is exactly how we are if we approach each day without spending time with the Lord. I am not being legalistic here. The only way we can grow in Jesus Christ and let him live through us is seeking him through the Bible and through prayer. If I desire to lead for Jesus Christ, I cannot neglect reading the Bible and prayer.

I'm not saying I couldn't win games if I neglected spending time with the Lord and used this extra time in preparing for practice or watching film. I am saying that I would not be effective in building God's kingdom. In Matthew, Jesus tells us, "For where your treasure is, there your heart will be also" (Matt. 6:21, ESV). If I wake up and my heart is focused on preparing to win, then that is my treasure. If I wake up and I spend time with God in order to get my heart focused on him, then God becomes my treasure.

See, it's real simple yet very complex. I must take ownership of my pursuit of Jesus Chris, and, therefore, my growth in him. The more I grow in Christ and become like him, the more effective I will become for his kingdom. Our salvation is 100 percent in Christ and his work on the cross. I also believe our growth in Christ and our impact on his kingdom has a lot to do with our pursuit of him. This has nothing to do with salvation; this is has everything to do with being a good worker for Jesus Christ. My desire is to lead my players for Jesus Christ. I cannot do this if I am not pursuing Christ through his word and prayer.

I am not saying that game and practice preparation is not critical as a coach. However, spending time each day seeking God through his word and prayer will empower us, with the Holy Spirit leading and guiding us in leading for Jesus Christ. I really don't think I have ever lost a game because of lack of preparation. We lose because we make mistakes. Spending time with God each day should never impact preparation. If it does, then I'm just being lazy with diligent preparation.

Therefore, I challenge you and me with this: do not give God crumbs of our time. Be intentional in spending time with Christ. You might have to go to bed early so you can spend quality time with the Lord; you might lose an hour of sleep; you might only get to watch film for thirty hours a week instead of thirty-five. Spend time solely with the Lord apart from a podcast of a sermon or a book written by a man. Spend time in the Word. Learn how to read it and ponder over it. As the Word says,

> For the word of God is living and active, sharper than any two-edged sword, piercing to the division of soul and of spirit, of joints and of marrow, and discerning the thoughts and intentions of the heart. (Heb. 4:12, ESV)

God has used men like John Piper, John MacArthur, and Andrew Murray in my life to influence me tremendously. But not one of these men's words are living and active like the word of God. I am often tempted to drive and pray or run and listen to a podcast in the place of sitting quietly before God, pursuing him. How enticing it is to be more efficient with our time. Don't let other things compete with the single most important part of your life—Jesus Christ. Don't hate me, but I am convicted this is absolutely wrong. Some days, it is necessary. However, most of our days should have a time when we can sit quietly before God, immersed in his word and in prayer. Do this and still pray while you drive and listen to podcasts while on your run. Immerse yourself in good books written by good Christian men. Even though these supplement our pursuit of Christ, they should not be how we do our devotions.

As I seek to not give God crumbs of my time and make sure he gets the best part of my day, I challenge myself with this thought: *If the God who created me, formed me, and causes my mind to work, if he desired to do so, could he not give me the perfect play call right when I need it?* Of course he could. I often have to remind myself to quit seeking to become the omniscient football coach. There is only One who is omniscient, and it is not attainable by anyone else! Therefore, I will be more diligent to sacrifice a little sleep and a little film watching to pursue the One who controls all things!

Just like the young man who walked into the weight room complaining about his teacher and grade, we too must take ownership of our relationship with Christ. What is it that hinders you from pursuing Christ? For me, it would be anything that has to do with winning as a football coach—watching film, thinking about practice execution, thinking about game strategy, thinking of ways to motivate my players, and on and on. These are good but can be distractions. I must put all distractions aside that hinder my pursuit of Christ. These things are not evil and not bad, but they must be second. I must take ownership of my time and my pursuits. Once again, I either control my actions or my actions control me.

Taking Ownership Pleases the Lord

I want to please the Lord. I was always scared to say such a thing because I was fearful people would label me as a person who believed I could earn God's favor and salvation. I clearly understand our salvation is from the Lord, and there is nothing I can do to add to this. However, scripture is clear—we can grieve the Holy Spirit and we can bless the Lord.

I want to consider the following passage from First Corinthians, written by the apostle Paul, as the basis for my logic:

> According to the grace of God given to me, like a skilled master builder I laid a foundation, and someone else is building upon it. Let each one take care how he builds upon it. For no one can lay a foundation other than that which is laid, which is Jesus Christ. Now if anyone builds on the foundation with gold, silver, precious stones, wood, hay, straw—each one's work will become manifest, for the Day will disclose it, because it will be revealed by fire, and the fire will test

> what sort of work each one has done. If the work that anyone has built on the foundation survives, he will receive a reward. If anyone's work is burned up, he will suffer loss, though he himself will be saved, but only as through fire. (1 Cor. 3:10–15, ESV)

This message is written to the believers, to the people who are going to heaven. Even though believers may be saved, there are works believers pursue that will be burned up and will inflict loss. I have no clue what that loss is and how that person will only be saved as "through fire." I just know the Bible clearly states believers who are saved can receive a reward and can suffer loss.

In my opinion, this is a call to focus on pursuing the things that build God's kingdom. I believe it is easy for us to have one hand in the world and the other doing God's work. I know I am guilty of this daily. However, I know this is why Paul tells Christians in Colossians to "seek the things that are above" and "set your minds on the things that are above, not on things that are on earth" (Col. 3:1–2, ESV). The things that we pursue on this earth that have no purpose for the kingdom of God are going to burn up; we are wasting our time with these things.

Now, I just spent the day helping my wife paint and clean up our backyard. I'm sure this has no kingdom value, but I also don't think this is an activity that is meaningless and will be burned up. Those are enjoyable things the Lord has given us to do. However, I spend a whole lot of time trying to win football games. If I do this to glorify myself and make tons of money, if I put worldly things in front of coaching to build Champions for Jesus Christ, these pursuits are going to burn.

I believe a coach can seek to win a state championship or a national championship, and it is all in how he pursues it that will make all the difference on whether that trophy burns or remains in heaven. I am saying a coach can be a believer and yet still be coaching in ways that some of his works are going to burn. I don't want this to happen to me. I want God to find my work valuable to the kingdom of God. No matter the level I coach or the money I make, I want my work to survive the fire. The Bible is clear that only the work we do with our eyes on Christ is going to be of any value.

Every day we can wake up, take ownership of our actions, and pursue Christ. As we pursue Christ, he will empower us to work in ways that produce fruit that will survive the fire, and therefore, these works will be worthy of a reward from the Lord. I find this highly motivating. You mean I can please the God of the universe, the Creator, Sustainer, and Redeemer of our souls? This fires me up. I could care less about this worldly stuff that is going to burn. I am pursuing Christ and his work!

I can only do this through Christ. I have to keep my eyes on Christ. I know I am fired up right now as I type this up. I also know my evil flesh apart from Christ. I will pursue my own glory and my own happiness in a heartbeat left to myself. But by the power of the Holy Spirit that works in me, I will build for his kingdom and for his glory.

A Prayer

O Lord, my Strength and my Rock—empower me to build for your kingdom. Empower me to take ownership of my actions. Empower me to pursue you with undivided dedication. Then, Lord, as you fill my heart, my soul, and my mind with your Holy Spirit, you will work in me to produce work that will not burn but stand the test of the fire you will put it through. I desire to please you, Lord. I desire this reward you discuss. I desire to please you, my God and my King.

Therefore, I do pray that the words of my mouth be acceptable in your sight. May nothing I say damage anyone, and may my speech always be gracious, loving, and kind. I pray the meditation of my heart be acceptable in your sight. Lord, I know you look down and see the intentions and the desires from the heart. From the desire of the heart come our actions. O Lord, my Rock and my Redeemer, may I bring you glory and honor with the intent of my heart and my actions. Amen.

7

WIN THE DAY!

IF YOU ARE A TRUE competitor, the pressure to perform and be the best can become suffocating. As I write this, many of the former players I coached are going through spring practice in college. Each one of these boys is competing for the starting job on the football team. Having played myself, I understand there are two things going on in their hearts: (1) they really do want to start on the football team and (2) pride is involved as they will be embarrassed if they do not. They will feel as if they are letting their parents, their coaches, their teammates, and the people from their hometown down.

The pressure they place upon themselves could damage their ability to perform. Instead of playing with a relentless desire to excel, they will play with a fear of failure. All of us understand the fear of failure. It is paralyzing. Instead of making things happen, we are scared to death to do anything. Focusing on Winning the Day helps us put things in perspective. Winning the Day is simply this thought process: I don't know what will come tomorrow and what happened yesterday is gone, but what I do have control over is giving my absolute best today!

Even though I don't know what will come tomorrow, I do know that what I do and accomplish today will impact my success tomorrow. So often we look into the future and get excited about an event. As a football coach, I could get excited about the next football season or on Monday be excited about the game on Friday night. However, dwelling on that game or football season does nothing to help my team be successful. The work we do each day will lead to our success in the future. We must treat each day like it's the championship game.

People often ask me what are goals are for the upcoming season. I know goals are important, but I have one major goal: Win the Day. I think it is common sense that a team is preparing to win a regional championship and a state championship. That is everyone's goal. If those aren't goals, then you might as well not even play the game. But having the goal doesn't make it happen. The only thing we can control in our life is working hard and preparing today. What happened yesterday is gone; the future is yet to come. We prepare for tomorrow by doing our best today.

As a coach, it is important that I focus on doing my best with the opportunity I have in this day the Lord has given me. I think it is human nature to focus on things that have no impact on the outcome of the game. When I first started coaching, I would spend many hours figuring out the height and weight of the defensive players. Sometimes I would turn on the film and see giants and be overcome with worry and anxiety. That stuff has no effect on the outcome of the game. I don't care if they are as big as a Mack truck; you still have to get in there and block them! We must train our minds to focus on the things that are going to help us win, not the things that make us lose heart.

I woke up and sent the text below to our boys we have playing in college. Like I mentioned, they are all started spring practice, and they feel pressure to win the starting job. Hopefully, you can see how

I broke it down into pieces they can control. We all can apply these principles to our life:

> Most of you guys are starting spring practice. You might feel a lot of pressure to perform. This can cause despair. This is where the "Win the Day" philosophy helps. God made each of us to do certain things and lead for him. All you can do is your best with what he has given you. If that is fourth, third, second, or first team— then so be it. All that matters is that you give your best. Learn how to give your best every single rep, and you will go far in life. It's your character that counts.
>
> As you practice, do these things and you will find favor with your coach: (1) do not use any words other than "yes sir" and "no sir"; (2) always be first to drills; (3) be relentless in your execution every snap; and (4) never let the seed of doubt creep into your mind.
>
> The power of Christ in your life is strength. Losers doubt; winners fight! Give Perfect Effort! I love you guys and am proud of you.

Win the Day for Christ

I pray these boys take the same desire and passion they are displaying in their quest to start on the football field into their pursuit of Jesus Christ. Football is a great tool God uses to teach passion and desire. We must never forget, we are made by God in his image for his glory and his honor. I pray all of those boys are successful on the football field, but what I desire most is they will pursue Christ with passion and desire each day so he can mold and shape them into Christian men. I desire they Win the Day for Christ!

It is relatively easy to see how focusing on the importance of each day will help us win in the sport we coach. I think it is even more important if we are going to be a champion for Jesus Christ. There are so many areas in which we can get distracted and lose our focus in our quest to be a Champion for Jesus Christ. It is imperative that we keep our eyes focused on Jesus Christ.

Jesus talks about this attitude in Matthew 6:33–34:

> But seek first the kingdom of God and his righteousness, and all these things will be added to you. Therefore do not be anxious about tomorrow, for tomorrow will be anxious for itself. Sufficient for the day is its own trouble. (ESV)

This is Jesus telling us to Win the Day! He tells us to focus on his kingdom and his righteousness and everything else will take care of itself because he is in control. There are many things that are going to come our way today, and we need to focus on accomplishing the task at hand. Tomorrow will take care of itself. Take care of today, and you will be fine tomorrow. Win the Day!

Notice I didn't say "Be lazy today and do nothing—trust God to take care of everything"? Nope! God calls each of us to work and to build. In fact, the work we have to do each day is a blessing from the Lord. It is his gift to us, and we can bless the Lord through this work. The Lord tells us to not be anxious for tomorrow so we can place our mind completely on the task at hand today. Anxiety is paralyzing, and this prohibits from being fruitful today.

The Lord also tells us to rejoice in each day: "This is the day that the Lord has made; let us rejoice and be glad in it" (Ps. 118:24, ESV). Each day the Lord gives us here on earth is a blessing and is used to build his kingdom. As a coach, I do this by investing in young men to build Champions for Jesus Christ. In this process, every single day is critical. I will rejoice in the opportunity God has given me today, and I will be glad in process of building Champions. Today matters. Today is a gift. I will give perfect effort today. Win the Day!

A Game Plan to Win the Day for Christ

The world probably thinks the "Win the Day for Christ" talk is foolish. I believe Christians often fail to realize there is a war going on that we cannot see. There is a war, and it is being waged by the prince of this world—Satan. Not only is Satan waging a war against God's kingdom, but we are also at war with our flesh and its desires. As coaches, we understand the importance knowing our opponent inside and out in order to effectively attack. How much more important is it for us to process and analyze the enemy in our battle to live for Jesus Christ in this sinful world.

Satan wants to destroy our relationship with Christ. He knows he is defeated, and he wants to take us all down with him. He hates Jesus and desires to destroy all the things that are important to him—things such as our family and our witness for Christ. I know the devil wants to destroy my marriage, as this will have a devastating impact on my witnessing for the Lord and my relationship with my son. We must remain completely focused on living for Christ each day as to not let the devil have a foothold in our life. As soon as we take our eyes off Christ, we will become blind to how we are drifting from him. We are not strong in and of ourselves, as the Word says, "So, if you think you are standing firm, be careful that you don't fall" (1 Cor. 10:12, NIV).

I have done my best to simplify the enemy and develop a strategy, and I think it is wise to meditate on this as we go throughout the day. This is strategy will help us Win the Day for Jesus Christ:

1. We Must Understand the Opponent

> The heart is deceitful above all things, and desperately sick; who can understand it. (Jer. 17:9, ESV).
> Behold, I was brought forth in iniquity, and in sin did my mother conceive me. (Ps. 51:5, ESV).

I am my opponent! I was born into sin. From birth, my heart has sought its own way. I have a desire to only please myself and seek glory for myself. In my sinful state, I do not desire God, and God has nothing of any value for me. I am blind to my sin, just like the sinful woman in Proverbs 5:6: "she does not ponder the path of life; her ways wander, and she does not know it" (ESV).

Even though Satan is coming after us, he is only using the desire we have for sin to entice us. Even though he desires to devour us, our biggest battle is our sinful hearts and flesh. God tells us in First John not to pursue the things of the world and he identifies these as "the desires of the eyes, the desires of the flesh and the pride of possessions" (1 John 2:16). We are born sinful, and apart from Christ, we are glory seekers and pleasure seekers. There is a reason the world's version of love is self-seeking. This is who we are in our sinful state.

God makes it clear about the intentions of our heart as he describes it as "desperately sick." There is no sin that each and everyone one of us in incapable of committing. Our hearts are not just sick, but they are desperately sick. Left to ourselves, we will desire more and more evil. We are all evil, and we are all born with an insatiable desire for sin.

2.   We Must Develop a Basic Strategy

> Purge me with hyssop, and I shall be clean;
> wash me, and I shall be whiter than snow.
> Let me hear joy and gladness;
> let the bones that you have broken rejoice.
> Hide your face from my sins,
> and blot out all my iniquities.
> Create in me a clean heart, O God,
> and renew a right spirit within me.
> Cast me not away from your presence,
> and take not your Holy Spirit from me.
> Restore to me the joy of your salvation,
> and uphold me with a willing spirit.
>   (Ps. 51:7–12, ESV)
> Search me, O God, and know my heart!
> Try me and know my thoughts!
> And see if there be any grievous way in me,
> and lead me in the way everlasting.
>   (Ps. 139:23–24, ESV)

As we just read about our opponent, it seems as if there is no hope. Praise God, we are not left to ourselves. We have hope and strength from our Lord and Savior, Jesus Christ. The blood of Jesus Christ has forgiven each of our sins. Through the cross, he has conquered death, and we now have access to God through Christ. He has sent his Holy Spirit to empower us that we may put to death the sinful man in us and live in the power of Jesus Christ.

We must put on Christ daily. Before we can do anything else, we must accept him as our Lord and Savior and repent of our sins against him. God will then create a clean heart within us. We will have a renewed desire to serve the Lord and live for him. God will empower us to understand our ways, and we will have a clear purpose in him.

3. The Offensive Strategy

> I have been crucified with Christ. It is no longer
> I who live but Christ who lives in me. And the
> life I now live in the flesh I live by faith in the
> Son of God, who loved me and gave himself
> for me. (Gal. 2:20, ESV)

In football, if the offense my team runs is going to be successful, there cannot be one selfish member on the field. I tell each kid they must die to their selfish agenda. Every running back wants the ball every time. Every quarterback wants to throw the ball every time. Every wide receiver wants the ball thrown to him all the time. (Praise the Lord for offensive linemen who just want to be on the field. They come to us already crucified to their selfishness.) However, in order to win, each one of those players at those positions must put those desires to death.

The wide receivers are going to have to block. The running back is not going to get the ball every time. The quarterback is not going to throw every time. They must put what is best for the team before what is best for them. They may not lead the state in certain categories, but their team will win. This is the greatest goal. But look, winning on the football field requires a group of young men willing to die to their selfish agenda and do what is best for the team with a great attitude.

If we are going to win for Christ, we must die to our sinful state and live in Jesus Christ. Yes, our flesh will still be at war within us, but we must constantly crucify these desires that flare up from our sin nature. The wide receiver, quarterback, and running back must constantly check their desire for personal accolades intruding on the greater good of the team. If we are going to be Champions for Jesus Christ, we must die to self!

4. The Defensive Strategy

> If then you have been raised with Christ, seek
> the things that are above, where Christ is, seated
> at the right hand of God. Set your mind on the
> things that are above, not on the things that
> are on earth. (Col. 3:1–2, ESV)

There are two things on which individual players must focus in order to have a great defense: (1) intensity in doing their job and (2) relentlessness in executing their assignment. We demand all our defensive players have their eyes on their assignment when the ball is snapped. The linebacker is most likely going to be keying the guard, and the guard's block will tell him what the play is and what he is supposed to do. There is nothing that makes me more mad than when I watch film and it is obvious the linebacker was not keying the guard. This happens when they are not focused on their assignment. When they do this, our whole defense messes up.

When all our guys are focused on their assignment and have their eyes in the right spot, we play great defense. When they get distracted, then we mess up. It's annoying! Christ gives us the same assignment if we are going to live for him in telling us to set our eyes on heaven. We are to set our eyes on heaven because where our eyes are, our minds are. As we set our minds on heaven, we see Christ, and he is our purpose. Just like when the linebacker takes his eyes off the guard, when we take our eyes of Christ, taking our eyes off our key, we get distracted and we make mistakes.

Therefore, our defensive strategy is to focus on our key—Jesus Christ. We will not be tempted by the desires of the world, the desires of the flesh, or the pride of possessions if we keep our eyes on Christ. It sounds easy, doesn't it? Yeah, I always wonder why we make mistakes on defense as well! It takes discipline, commitment, and pain to daily keep our eyes on Christ. However, we must strive to give Championship effort in keeping our eyes on Christ.

5. Never Quit

> And we know that for those who love God all things work together for good, for those who are called according to his purpose. (Rom. 8:28, ESV)

No matter what happens in our life, in time of success and in times of total despair, we can take comfort that Jesus Christ loves us and is using every situation for our good. He will use time of despair and calamity to shape and mold us; he will use times of success and happiness as a blessing to our hearts. We can always rest assured nothing will separate us from the love of Jesus Christ (Rom. 8:31–39).

Therefore, may we all pursue Christ with all diligence. May we make him the most important part of our day and therefore our lives so we may be Champions for Jesus Christ and God can use us to build Champions for Jesus Christ.

A Prayer

> O Lord, how great and powerful you are! You are my King. I am your servant. Empower me to do your will. Lord, fill me with your Holy Spirit so I may be effective for your kingdom today. Tomorrow is not promised, and yesterday is gone. Today is a gift from you to be used to build your kingdom. Today, may I invest in each soul that you place before me through a loving and encouraging attitude. Use me to challenge each young man I coach and every

man with whom I work, to become all they can be in Christ.

Lord, the work we do today will impact our success tomorrow. This is true, both in the profession you have given us and in our growth in Christ. Keep our eyes focused upon you and living for you. Do not let us get distracted by the pressures and desires of this world. Help us not to be anxious about tomorrow for tomorrow will be anxious for itself. Sufficient for the day is its own trouble. Help me to win today, Lord. Winning today is simply seeking first your kingdom and your righteousness. You have the power to give us all that we need. May we trust in you. As we go forward today, Lord, teach us more about yourself. Teach us about Winning the Day for Jesus Christ. This is all that matters. How great you are! Lead us, Lord! Lead us! Amen.

8

NO EXCUSES

I SAW A GREAT QUOTE about missing practice: "The only time missing practice is excused is for your funeral." I know that is a little extreme, but a coach said it because people are full of excuses for why we cannot do things. I am sure this coach got sick and tired of hearing all the different reasons why someone is going to be late or miss practice. This is a good way to let everyone know there is no excuse for missing practices. Get tough and suck it up.

"No Excuses" is not just a motto that I preach to my players; I preach it to myself. I wake up every day and do not want to do certain things. I teach class all day and have 120–160 students that I have to control, motivate, and instruct. By 3:30 p.m., time for practice, I can be a little worn out. I have to train my brain to be motivated and embrace practice. My players have to get my absolute best from 3:30 p.m. to 6:30 p.m., even though I am drained by 3:30 p.m. It does not matter. I could come up with great excuses to loaf as a coach at practice. I have to bring my best. I have to find my best. My players and people around me will respond to my attitude and effort. No Excuses.

As a father and a husband, it is no different. I come home from work, and I am tired and worn out. I'd love to just sit down on the couch and do nothing. I've been around people all day, and I do not really want to talk and play. However, I walk in the door, and my little boy gets a big ol' smile on his face and he is ready to play! His mom is happy I walk in the door because she wants a break! The couch is appealing, but I have a duty as a father to embrace my son and spend time with him and give mom a break. No Excuses.

By the time I get home, I'm worn out and I've listened to people all day long. The last thing I want to do is make my brain function by listening some more. However, my wife hasn't talked to anyone but a babbling one-year-old. I need to lock into her, pay her attention, and listen to her. Boy, I am a failure at this often, but I want to be better. I strive to be better. There is really no excuse for when I ignore her but selfishness and laziness!

Now it probably looks like I am boasting in my being the perfect coach, husband, and father. Absolutely not! I used each example above because each is extremely important to me, and I strive to improve daily. I fail consistently. However, instead of making excuses for my failure, I readily admit I failed. Once I can admit I have failed, I can also start to plan on how not to fail in the future. My wife will tell you that I don't talk to her enough, I don't listen to her enough, and I don't cherish her enough. I'm trying to be better each day. I want to be a better husband, father, and coach. I am not perfect, but I strive to be better each day. I try not to make excuses for my failures but instead analyze them and try and do better.

We must understand the root of all failure is a battle of the will. Players come to me all the time, and they tell me they can't. I tell them to not tell me they can't but, rather, tell me they won't. When they tell me "I can't," what they are really saying is "I am too selfish"; "I have other priorities"; "or "I'm too lazy." They can do whatever they want to do. They will stay up until midnight talking to their girlfriends on the phone or watching a movie, but they won't do that in studying for a test (some might). So I tell them, "Quit saying you can't do something—just tell me you won't." They can do it. If they don't, it's just they're lazy and making excuses. I am the same way. I preach this to myself! I fail daily! No Excuses!

Apathy

The theologian John Stott defined *apathy* as "the acceptance of the unacceptable." Apathy is when the excuses we make begin to be okay. Maybe I'm crazy, but when I sit back and watch kids miss a day or two of school because they are sick, you know what they realize? They can miss more days of school because they are sick. Now, don't get me wrong, I realize kids get sick and there are days they must miss due to severe illnesses. However, I see kids who, at least once a week, don't feel good. It has become acceptable for them to miss school. Of course they are going to make an excuse for why they don't want to come to school—they don't feel good. I don't think I've woken one time in my life and felt good unless I was on vacation.

When you play football for me, the standard is, if you miss a day of practice during the week, you aren't playing on Friday night. (Now there are exceptions but not many.) You say that is unfair, what if a kid is sick and just can't practice? It is absolutely amazing how I cannot think of a starter who has missed a day of practice unless they were severely sick. I haven't either. You know why. Because there is a standard. Missing practice is unacceptable. They know in their minds they have to get up and come. If they want Friday night, they have to pay the price: they don't get sick. To me, it is proof that apathy is the "acceptance of the unacceptable."

Now, there have been times when a kid has been at home with a 103-degree temperature and was truly sick. Of course I am sympathetic when it comes to this. However, kids must learn to push through the sniffles and not feeling good. It's a rare day when they are going to wake up and feel good and be excited about going to school and then a three-hour practice. But to defeat apathy, we must learn to control our attitudes and our minds. It is why we have the "Win the Day" philosophy. It is why we preach "No Excuses!" Get up and get going. Don't let this day defeat you! It's you versus this day. Who is going to win? Are you going to make some silly excuse like you have a headache, you have the sniffles? Get up and get going! Attack the day! Win the Day! Do not let apathy overtake your mind!

Nehemiah Makes No Excuses

Whenever I need encouragement to not make excuses, I like to go and read the story of Nehemiah. God called Nehemiah to go build the Walls of Jerusalem. This was no wall like the one in someone's backyard. This wall stretched around a whole city for miles. The wall was to fend off the enemy. You can imagine the wall that Nehemiah was told by God to go and restore. This in itself was a challenging task.

Not only did Nehemiah have to rebuild this wall; he had to do it with enemies at every side. In fact, it was so bad that he and his men had to build with one hand and keep their knives in the other. Can you imagine having to motivate a group of men to build a wall while their lives were at stake? I see three major challenges for Nehemiah: (1) the wall was huge and repairing it is a very daunting task; (2) he and his men had enemies on every side that wanted to kill them for repairing the wall; and (3) Nehemiah had to be a great leader of men to motivate them to continue building each day in the face of persecution.

If you really study Nehemiah and what was going on during this time, you understand he probably wanted to quit every single day. He had very good excuses for quitting he could have used. I can see him praying to God and saying some of the following excuses, "Lord, I am tired and worn out trying to motivate these men. Each day I have to encourage them and motivate them, as they fear for their lives. I am tired and I have no more in me." Or "Lord, this wall is just too big. I thought we could do it, but we have to work all day every day. I am tired and worn out for this wall is too large, this task too complicated." Or "Lord, I have people trying to kill me for doing your work. I was good with all this until my life became at stake. That is taking it too far. You need to find another guy."

The list of excuses in which Nehemiah could have contrived is endless. As a coach, I have to deal with kids missing practice because of the sniffles or someone has a bruise. There is always an excuse to not do something! However, Nehemiah never made an excuse. He had a job to do from the Lord, and he was going to accomplish by the power of God, which powerfully worked in him!

In chapter 6 of Nehemiah, we read about a group of men who were trying to lure Nehemiah into a meeting where they were going to harm him or kill him. When Nehemiah would not go to the meeting because he knew it was a trap, they started to falsely accuse Nehemiah of treason. The accusation of treason would get everyone flustered and put Nehemiah in trouble with the people; they could rebel against his leadership. Man, every day Nehemiah had to contend with this stuff. He is trying to do the Lord's work and rebuild the wall but has to manage all these attacks and threats upon his life each day. It was a full-time job just to manage the threats and attacks, much less build a wall! Boy, did he have some valid excuses to quit.

I can see him being a little discouraged and disheartened. He had two directions he could go at this point:

1. "Lord, I'm done. I can't do this. I love you and I want to be your servant and be a leader for your work. But I just can't handle all of this. I'm sorry."
2. "Lord, I can't do this, but you can. Empower me with your Holy Spirit and help me keep my eyes upon the mission. Help me to keep my eyes focused upon you, the One who is able!"

Nehemiah chose the second option. He didn't quit. He didn't make excuses. In fact, amid all the chaos, he spoke these powerful words: "But now, O God, strengthen my hands" (Neh. 6:9, ESV).

Nehemiah is just one of many examples in the Bible of men who were called to perform a challenging task. These men all had great excuses to quit, but they did not. From studying these men—foremost of which is the work of Jesus Christ—I have realized excuses are annoying to the Lord. He does not want to hear us say "can't." He wants us to seek him with all our might, trust in him, and let him work through us. Truly, we are right when we say, "I can't." But we are wrong to not say, "I can't, but God, who has promised to work in me and through me, can! I will seek him with all diligence so that his power may mightily work in me." No Excuses.

I Did Not Say "No Failure"

So often everyone is looking for some quick-and-easy scheme to become great. No one wants to go through the adversity of trying and failing. Just because you work real hard and are bought into the "No Excuses" philosophy, this does not mean instant success. This does not mean you will never lose. You will lose daily. You will struggle. You will fail. But what you cannot do is make excuses when you fail. You have to get right back up and keep on working, keep on pursuing excellence.

I love this saying: "The darkest part of the night is right before the sun rises." I believe true failure is quitting. Think about that in your personal life. Are you struggling? Are you tired, worn out, and want to quit? Are you amid the darkest part of the night? The sun is going to come up. You have to keep on plugging and keep on working. Do not give up! When you quit trying, you are a failure. When you fail yet persevere, then you are a winner!

Guard you heart against making excuses. Win each day! No Excuses.

The End Result for Excuse Makers

These passages from Proverbs motivate me not to make excuses:

> I passed by the field of a sluggard,
> by the vineyard of a man lacking sense,
> and behold, it was all overgrown with thorns;
> the ground was covered with nettles,
> and its stone wall was broken down.
> Then I saw and considered it;
> I looked and received instruction.
> A little sleep, a little slumber,
> a little folding of the hands to rest,
> and poverty will come upon you like a robber,
> and want like an armed man. (Prov.
>   24:30–34, ESV)

Here is my interpretation of these verses: A man passes by the field and a vineyard of a sluggard. A sluggard is a lazy and worthless man who thinks he knows everything but, in reality, has no sense. This field and vineyard were overgrown with thorns and nettles. At one point, it was obvious there was a fruitful field and vineyard, but no one took care of it now. The stone wall was all broken down, and no one cared.

I believe a hardworking man who built it from the ground up and took great care of it once owned this estate. But he left it to his children's care, and they were lazy. They didn't have to work to build it, and with their dad gone, they have no idea how to work. They are lazy. They are sluggards. Their entire lives they had things handed to them, and they have no idea how to work hard each day. They are pleasure seekers and do not understand the concept of hard work. This was once a beautiful estate, and now it is appalling to look at because no one has taken care of it.

The man walking by saw it and received a little instruction from its appearance: "Go ahead and sleep and don't work. Make excuses for why you can't do things. Complain about how you don't feel good. Pursue pleasure and happiness at the expense of hard work and discipline. Waste the talent and treasures you have been given. Go ahead, be lazy and poverty will come upon you quickly, and you will be craving for food and money like a robber."

I feel like the Lord is warning me through this proverb, saying, "Young man, Win the Day! No Excuses!"

No Excuses in Pursuing Christ

Salvation is totally and completely the work of Jesus Christ. We can add nothing to our salvation, and we cannot take ownership of any of it. We are saved by the grace of God. There is nothing we can do to earn our salvation. In fact, man does not even seek salvation. Apart from the work of Jesus Christ, we are dead in our sins and have no desire for God or for forgiveness. Therefore, salvation is from the Lord.

However, sanctification refers to what happens after salvation. I believe God has given us responsibility for our sanctification, which is our growth in Christ. Even though God puts the desire in our hearts to love and serve him and he inclines our hearts to his testimonies, we are responsible to put forth the effort to seek him through his word and prayer.

In this pursuit, we must be careful we do not become so busy with this world that we neglect the kingdom of God. In fact, we should be so busy with the kingdom of God that we neglect this world. I find warning of making excuses in my pursuit of Christ from the parable about the great banquet in Luke 14.

The servant was sent out, and he was inviting people to the great banquet. The banquet represents God inviting us into his kingdom and being his people. So many had excuses for why they could not come: "I have bought a field, and I must go out and see it. Please have me excused." Another said, "I have bought five yoke of oxen, and I go to examine them. Please have me excused." And another said, "I have married a wife, and therefore I cannot come" (Luke 14:12–24, ESV).

All these serve as excuses we all make in our pursuit of Christ. When we don't pursue Christ as our number 1 passion in this life, what we are really saying is this: "Lord, I have other priorities in this world rather than you. I am way more important than your kingdom. I don't trust you for one second in handling the things of the world for me. I will seek you when I have time. You are important to me but not my top priority."

I challenge us all that we would pursue Christ and his kingdom with undivided dedication. Let nothing in this world distract us from our goal to live a life wholly devoted to Christ. As we set our minds on Christ and trust in him with all our hearts and minds, we can be confident he will lead us in the way everlasting and he will take care of our earthly concerns. The Creator of the universe can surely take care of our needs. We are left with No Excuses in our pursuit of Christ.

A Prayer

O Lord, my Savior and my Rock—help me not make any excuses in this life! Most importantly, let me never make excuses for why I cannot pursue you and your kingdom. Lord, I know I am full of excuses when it comes to pursuing you. Please forgive me. Just like the excuses mentioned before, I let the business of everyday life hinder my pursuit of your kingdom. Grant me the wisdom and the ability to pursue you instead of the things of this world. Let there be no excuses in me as to why I cannot pursue you and be used to build your kingdom. Lead me, O Lord, and direct my steps. Help me to diligently seek you with all my heart, my soul, and my mind. I have no excuse for not pursuing you with unbridled fervor and passion each day, except apathy and laziness. May this diligence in seeking you carry over to being diligent in leading for Jesus Christ with my family and through the job with which you have blessed me. Destroy excuses in me, Lord. Amen.

9

PERFECT EFFORT

PERFECT EFFORT IS A PRODUCT of intensity, commitment, consistency, and execution. As a math equation, it would look like this:

$$\text{Intensity} + \text{Commitment} + \text{Consistency} + \text{Execution} = \text{Perfect Effort}$$

It is easy to be intense and to execute once or twice; however, when you throw the variables *commitment* and *consistency* in the equation, you gain the word *perfect*. Perfect Effort is giving your absolute best all the time.

Most people can give great effort when they feel like it. Very few people can give great effort when they don't feel good or when adversity strikes. This is why I don't say to my players, "Give effort." No! That is not good enough—"Give Perfect Effort!" When we give Perfect Effort, we will then maximize all the ability God has given us.

In reality, we have no control over how successful we will become doing anything. So much of success is outside of our control. I'm five eleven, and I played offensive line. I sure did work hard and tried to be my absolute best, but you just don't see many five-eleven offensive linemen in the NFL. I'm pretty sure there isn't one. I had no control over the height variable! The only thing I had absolute control over in my life was my attitude and my effort. They directly correlate with each other. The better attitude I have, the better effort I will give.

I cannot ask young men to play the perfect game. This is the goal and this is what we prepare for every single day, but it is impossible to play the perfect game. There will be mistakes. However, I can ask them to give perfect effort. Giving perfect effort results in maximizing every variable within our control. I do not give our players a goal board that has numeric variables. When we throw numbers into things, we often get into things we really have no control over. However, I try and quantify effort.

Quantifying Effort

In football, in order to quantify effort, I have had to look and find the variables that we have complete control over. In our athletic development program, I have tried to do the same thing. We all have seen the T-shirts that state, "Effort takes no talent." In our lives, we have variables that take no talent yet require great effort. We must identify these.

When I watch our defense, I am looking for variables to judge and critique:

1. Are our players aligned correctly?
2. Do our players execute their assignment with the proper technique?
3. Do our players pursue the football relentlessly?
4. Do our players use the proper tackling technique?

If you break down the defense into those specific controlled variables and you grade your players on these variables, you will win all the time when you have better players. You will win a whole bunch of games even when you don't have the better players because your players "out-effort" the other team. Therefore, for me, it is imperative I try and quantify effort and grade it out to the best of my ability.

We do the same thing in the weight room as we try and develop athletes. I have a commitment chart with each player's name written down. The sole purpose of this commitment chart is to give a check if a kid works out each day of the week. Consistency is the first thing I need to work on with each player for them to grow as athletes. There is nothing worse in the world than a kid that shows up on Monday and Friday to work out but misses Tuesday, Wednesday, and Thursday. They will not get better doing this. So if they can see a check for the days they come, they can see whether they contain the first ingredient for success—consistency.

With this chart, I am measuring an aspect of perfect effort—did you show up and come to the weight room today? It is my job to demand intensity and push them and challenge them once they get to the weight room. But they are in control of showing up; I can't control that. Their commitment to showing up and being on time requires effort. Therefore, this is something I can grade and judge. Their consistency proves their commitment. That is why I call it a "commitment chart." Commitment requires effort. Showing up takes no talent but requires effort.

It would be foolish for me to judge each player according to his or her natural abilities. I could test at the end of each quarter, and there are certain kids who do not have to lift everyday in order to be stronger and more athletic than everyone else. To the kid who has God-given strength and athleticism, he only has to show up during testing time, and he will have better results than everyone else. So if all I am charting are the end results, I am missing out on making the great athletes even better.

By simply creating a chart that measures commitment, I have created an environment where hard work and discipline become core values. We don't glory in God-given talent; we glory in work ethic—in the ability to give effort in order to maximize one's ability each and every day. Every player is held to the same standard no matter of ability. They must come in and work out today in order to get the check. If you don't care about getting the check for today, then we have character issues—you don't want to work; you don't want to give effort. Eventually, a guy like this is going to make us lose.

No One Works Harder

When I first started coaching, I wanted to instill in our young players a desire for hard work and discipline. I had no idea if we were working harder than any other team or not, but I know I wanted our boys to believe they were working harder than every other team in the country. If I could get them passionate about outworking everyone, I knew they would give me all they had all the time! Over the course of time, this became giving Perfect Effort.

I quit saying "No One Works Harder" because it isn't true. I discuss with our boys there are a lot of schools who excel at the game of football because they work extremely hard year round. We have to give Perfect Effort every single day in order to compete and stay with these schools. In reality, I do not control whether or not we are working harder because I have no control over those schools. But, as a collective group, at my school, we do control giving Perfect Effort each and every day. If we do give Perfect Effort, then we must be working at least as hard as other schools giving Perfect Effort.

By focusing on Perfect Effort, we are focusing on an area of our life in which we are completely in control. When we focus on outworking someone else, we get into areas that cannot be measured and we have no idea if it is true or not. We also become consumed with someone else other than the variables we control. Perfect Effort empowers my players and me to do the best of our ability. It allows us to become the very best we can become. There is no stress or anxiety involved because the person we are competing against is ourselves.

When we can conquer ourselves and learn to push ourselves beyond natural limits, I believe there is no end to what we can accomplish. This is the root of why we discuss giving Perfect Effort. It can be applied to anything we do—for the boys I coach, the classroom, the weight room, the football field, their leadership, and, most importantly, their relationship with Christ.

Perfect Effort Requires Commitment

What a great concept, right, Perfect Effort? Giving perfect is not easy, and most will never even get close. The first ingredient for giving Perfect Effort is commitment. With the boys I coach and with adults, they all have the desire to do something and be successful, few will commit to anything. The following is a letter LSU sent out a long time ago to every high school football coach in the southeast about commitment:

> The Pain of Commitment
> Commitment can be painful.
> It is in the possibility for pain that commitment
>   finds its meaning and its power.
> Of what value would commitment be if it did
>   not have its price?
> Choose your commitments.
> Expect painful times.
> Be ready to make sacrifices.
> Be ready to see it through.

We all know commitment isn't easy. It is important we seek to give Perfect Effort in all that we do, but I do want to give a warning here to everyone: never commit to something and let it consume you that it will destroy the things that are important to God. Our wives, our children, and the pursuit to build God's kingdom are the most important things in the eyes of God. We must make sure we are applying Perfect Effort to the pursuit of these things. If you want to practice commitment, start with your family!

Perfect Effort Requires Consistency

I think commitment is a matter of the heart. Commitment is the desire. Consistency is the action. I can tell how committed a player is by their participation in our off-season workout program. I have kids every year that come up to me in January and tell me they are going to commit to playing football the next football season. Then, I hardly ever see them in the weight room in the off-season. They show up for a few days, and then they disappear. In their hearts, they want to commit and be a part of the team. Unfortunately, they have no control of their actions, and they cannot consistently train. Their ability to show up and train proves their commitment level.

It goes back to the quote "Your actions speak so much louder than your words." At the very least, Perfect Effort commands consistency. If a man will not show up and be at work, he is deemed lazy and worthless. I certainly do not want the kids who will not discipline themselves to be at off-season workouts to be on the team I coach. The inability to be consistent in working, much less giving Perfect Effort, proves these young men lack the ability to discipline themselves to accomplish a task.

There is never a day we are going to get up and get excited about waking up and going to work. However, we can wake up and embrace the work that is to be had that day. We can rejoice in the fact that we have the ability to work and even have work to do. As we change our attitude about work, we can then start to be consistent with our daily work habits. This is a vital lesson I try and teach to the boys I coach. If

I can empower them with the ability and willingness to work, I believe God has used me in a mighty way in their life.

Perfect Effort Requires Intensity

Once we throw intensity in with consistency, we then have the key variables for Perfect Effort. I spend a whole lot of energy every single day just trying to get boys to commit and then be consistent in showing up. Once I see they are consistent, which proves to me they are bought into what I am trying to do (which is to make them better), I then start attacking their intensity.

There is a difference between the man who shows up and just tries to get through the day and the man who shows up and tries to Win the Day! Intensity is focused effort. So when the boys show up in the off-season and work to become better athletes, I demand they push themselves on every single rep. I've got to push them to be intense in everything they do while they are with me.

Just imagine two teams preparing for a football game. One team just shows up to practice and goes through the motions to get through the day. There is no intensity and no passion to really get better. The kids are there, and therefore, a team exists. However, the coach does not demand intensity, and the players don't give it. They have talent but lack intensity at practice. The other team is working their tails off and giving focused effort every single rep. They are preparing in practice like each day is game day. This team is fully aware that what they do Monday through Thursday determines their success on Friday.

All talent being equal, which team do you think wins? Work is important, but it does not have much impact on our success. Yes, a man might get paid for just showing up to work, but it won't be long before his employer sees he adds no value to the organization. An employer is always looking for the guy who is a difference maker. The difference maker brings intensity to work. It is the intensity with which we work that will make all the difference.

Perfect Effort Requires Execution

There is a progression toward giving Perfect Effort. Commitment, consistency, and intensity are the three we have discussed so far. In my job, I have to get the boys to be consistent and intense when they come to the weight room and practice. Once I get those two things, I can really start to harp on them about their execution. Execution is all the little details that determine maximizing one's true potential.

As a coach, I am obsessed with execution on the football field. We can be out there consistently working with intensity, but if we are executing wrong, we are going to lose. If the kids are not executing their technique and assignments correctly every single rep at practice, we are wasting our time as coaches and, worse, our player's time. It is the same in the weight room as I develop these young men—we must execute our lifts correctly with correct form. We must have great execution in what we do to maximize our results.

The biggest issue I see with execution is laziness. We do not want to do the things that are hard and cause pain. I see it all the time with squats. People don't want to squat all the way down and execute a squat correctly because it is more painful than doing a half squat. The problem, though, is that the half squat doesn't do anything. It isn't making the player better. Success requires pain. Executing properly can be painful at times.

Perfect Effort Is a Heart Issue

Even though I have a formula for Perfect Effort, at the end of day, it is a heart issue. Commitment, consistency, intensity, and the desire to execute properly are all conceived within the heart. As a coach, I try and do everything in my power to ignite the flame of desire within the hearts of my players. With some, I just have to light the match; with a few, I have to fan the burning fire; and with others, I have to bring the fire and be the oil.

I want to motivate my players to be motivated from within. I tell them each year that if I am having to pull them every day, we are in trouble. But if all I have to do is push them, then we are going to have a great year. To me it's a matter of intrinsic motivation versus extrinsic motivation. I want kids that are motivated from the inside. Yes, I understand it is my job as a leader to be able to motivate the ones who need it. I will do my best, but I labor with great pain trying to find something that ignites the flame within that kid who needs constant prodding and pushing. I completely understand that my team will take on my intensity, but at some point, the kids have to be able to push themselves if we are going to be a great team.

It is because of this I really hate punishing kids for not working hard. I desperately want the kids to desire to be great from within. If I have to bring punishment into the equation, then I'm exhausting my resources of extrinsic motivation. I constantly think about how I can motivate my players to want to work. I am perfectly happy being the spark plug or the match. But, man, when I have to bring the motivation, bring the fire and the oil, every single day—we aren't going to be a good football team.

I absolutely love coaching kids who come in and give me their absolute best each and every single day. These are the kids of whom I can just fan their flame. A positive word here and there fuels them for weeks because they already have all the desire in their heart to be great. Perfect Effort might as well be their middle name. The desire and the motivation to excel come from within their hearts. When I have a team full of these kids, I can promise you I will have a great time coaching!

I love these kids so much that I give out an award called the Perfect Effort award. I could usually give it to way more kids than I do, but it always goes to the kids who didn't receive as much recognition as some others but their attitude and effort are second to none. In fact, without these kids, we wouldn't win football games; their desire and passion feeds onto everyone else. I think these kids make the kids who have more athletic talent better.

Perfect Effort in Our Pursuit of Christ

Just how I sit back and judge and monitor the hearts of my players, the Lord judges and monitors our hearts. We are but dust, and we are sinners. God understands this. We are going to mess up, and we are going to fail. God understands this. However, God is looking in our hearts, and he sees if we are truly motivated by our love for him and have a desire to serve him. In fact, scripture is clear that God judges our hearts. He tells the prophet Samuel, "Man looks on the outward appearance, but the LORD looks on the heart" (1 Sam. 16:7, ESV).

He tells Jeremiah this about the people of Israel: "I the LORD search the heart and test the mind, to give every man according to his ways, according to the fruit of his deeds" (Jer. 17:10, ESV). I wish I could look into the hearts of my players, but I can't. Their actions tell me a lot, but I can never see what is in their hearts with my eyes. God can. He looks into our hearts, and he sees our desires. He can see if we truly have a heart that desires to serve him and live for him wholly.

As King David is repenting of his sin, he prays to God with the following words:

> For you will not delight in sacrifice, or I
> would give it;
> you will not be pleased with a burnt offering.
> The sacrifices of God are a broken spirit;
> a broken and contrite heart, O God, you will not
> despise. (Ps. 51:16–17, ESV)

God does not care about what comes out of our mouths or our actions. Many people preach a good message and do what seem to be great deeds in the name of Jesus Christ, but their hearts are far from God. King David knew that God didn't want an outward appearance of repentance. God wanted a broken spirit and heart. God wants to desire him from within our hearts. He wants men and women who serve him with a whole heart, mind, and soul. Only God can see what is in our hearts. May we strive to give Perfect Effort in our pursuit of Jesus Christ.

A Prayer

O Lord, I am a sinful man, and I fail miserably to live up to your holy law and commands each day. But, my God and King, you know my heart and you know my desire. You know that I desire to live for you and serve you every single minute of each day. I mess up, Lord. I say and do things I should not. I praise you for your forgiveness. You look down from your throne, and you can see the desires of my heart. You see that my heart is wholly devoted to you. You see, Lord, that I give Perfect Effort in pursuit of you.

Lord, you desire sacrifices that come from a broken spirit and broken heart. O Lord, please continue to break me of my sinfulness. I desire that my whole heart be completely yours. May my heart and soul bow at your feet in humble submission to your will. Lord, may your Holy Spirit fill me and lead me so that I may give Perfect Effort in my pursuit of loving you and living for you. Forgive me of my sins and my iniquities. Continue to refine me into your image. Do not hold my sin against me. Forgive me and lead me in the way everlasting. My God, my King, and my Savior—how great thou art! Help me to give Perfect Effort in pursuit of you. Amen.

10

HUMILITY

IN MY OFFICE, I HAVE the following verse up on my wall: "You save a humble people, but your eyes are on the haughty to bring them down" (2 Sam. 22:28, ESV). This verse stands as a guard for me to not think much of myself. As I guard my heart against pride and arrogance, I also try and instill a spirit of humility in everyone involved in our football program—players, coaches, parents, and fans. All that we have and all that we are is Christ. I pray the Lord protect us from boasting in ourselves and seeking the glory of man.

The opposite of humility is pride, arrogance, and haughtiness. These things destroy a team. Always trying to maintain the "Win the Day" mind-set, I always tell myself and my team, "No one cares what you did yesterday, and you have not accomplished anything yet tomorrow. Therefore, let's go to work today!" If we sit around boasting in what we accomplished yesterday, that leaves us full of ourselves. We start to think we are invincible. We quit working hard. We lose our focus and our hunger for the work required today, as we are still living in the accomplishments of yesterday. Failure is lurking!

You will often here a coach say, "Success breeds success." When a team starts winning, they are more likely to keep winning because they have found confidence. Confidence is not pride. It is an attitude of belief in oneself and one's abilities. Confidence looks like this: "If I work hard and keep my mind focused on improving each day, I know I can be successful. I will continue to work hard and improve each day. I will give my all come game time, and I believe I will win. This winning is a result of hard work and determination in training." There is no danger in confidence, and it is healthy.

However, if left unchecked, confidence can become pride. Pride thinks this without even realizing it: "I don't have to work very hard and be diligent because I am great. No one can beat me. This team is lucky to have me. I will just show up and go through the motions at practice, and come game time, I will shine. Victory is always mine!" Yes, you can see the foolishness of these words. However, the prideful person does not process they are thinking this way; they just become this way. These thoughts are way down deep in their subconscious, and they are just reacting to these beliefs. Now, I will say there are actually people who understand they think this way and are just plain prideful at their core. I don't know if there is any hope for this man!

How often do we see a team have a huge win against a highly ranked opponent only to turn around and get upset by a lower-ranked opponent the following week? It happens all the time. What happens is a team loses their focus. They can't get over the big win and get their minds wrapped around the next opponent. The pride of the big win carries over into the preparation for the next opponent. It's so hard for this team to focus, as they still want to enjoy the pride in their big victory. However, the next opponent has laser focus in their preparation—an upset is brewing!

Because of this, I think it is prudent to enjoy a victory for that night and maybe a little the next morning. Any more than that, and pride will creep in and destroy our desire to work for the next opponent. We must remain humble in victory. For me, I like to enjoy it for a little while, as a lot of hard work went into being able to win. However, quickly I must put it behind me and prepare for my next opponent with this mentality: "My success yesterday is fleeting, and I have accomplished nothing yet in the future. Therefore, it is time to go to work today!"

Humility in Our Work

If I am to be a Champion for Jesus Christ and, as a leader, build Champions for Jesus Christ, I must constantly seek to be humble. All that we are and all that we have is from the Lord. We are all dependent upon our Creator to be our Provider. The humble man realizes God is his Creator, Sustainer, and Savior. We have life because God wills it. I am nothing; Christ is everything.

As we work hard for success, I believe it is important we understand the value of hard work, balanced with total dependence upon the Lord. God has given us the responsibility to work hard and cultivate the land. In Genesis, God recounts creating Adam and the responsibility he placed upon him: "The LORD God took the man and put him in the Garden of Eden to work it and keep it" (Gen. 2:15, ESV). Work is a blessing from the Lord and was created for our enjoyment. We should work hard to be successful with the responsibilities God has given us. There is no sin in desiring to be successful and working to be successful. In fact, this honors God.

With our hard work, it is imperative we pray and ask God to bless our work. We must understand that everything comes from the Lord. He has created all things. He makes all things work. As we pray the Lord to bless our work, we must approach him with the correct attitude.

First, as we approach the Lord in prayer, we are doing so with a heart of submission. We know God is the Creator of all things and we know he loves us and cares for us. We can trust him to give us what we need, according to his purposes and for his glory. Second, prayer for our daily work shows complete dependence upon God. This honors God. It acknowledges and praises him as our Creator and Provider.

When we work hard and strive for success apart from prayer, we leave God completely out of the process. We quickly start to do things for our benefit and our glory. Our mission and focus becomes to build our own empire so man may praise and honor us—God despises this. God desires a humble people who work hard for his glory and his honor. Therefore, in all that we do, we should work hard and seek God with all our hearts, minds, and souls in the process.

We must understand that we work for the glory of God—God is the reason we do what we do. He is central. We do not work hard for our own glory. We do not work hard and let God be a piece of the process. God is the process. It is imperative that in all that we do, we do it completely for God. So many people want to work hard and have their professional lives for themselves. After all, the Bible gives some great instruction that will help people be successful in their professional lives. These principles, if applied, will surely help us be successful.

Even if we follow godly principles and ideals in our work yet do not make Christ the reason we work, we will become prideful and arrogant. We will quickly look to acknowledge our discipline and commitment as the reason we are successful. This was the pride of the Pharisees in the Bible. They boasted in their good works and their discipline in godliness. However, their hearts were evil, and they served only themselves. As we make Christ the reason for all that we do, our hearts become captivated in him. When Christ has our hearts, then he can work through us.

True Humility

True humility begins when our eyes are truly opened by the Holy Spirit and we see ourselves for what we truly are—sinful and finite. We are born a sinful people seeking our own way and our own glory. One of the curses of sin is we all are headed toward death. Our lives are finite and our days are numbered. These two facts lead us to surrender all to the one who is infinite and sinless, Jesus Christ. Humility is counting ourselves as insignificant and surrendering all that we are and all that we do to Jesus Christ. Through this, we will surrender ourselves to the service of others, just as Jesus Christ did in his life here on earth.

We have life and breathe because the Lord has given this to us. Our heart beats because the Lord allows it. How is it that we can boast of anything? For the heart surgeon, he or she has an amazing mind, and this is given to them from the Lord. For the amazing athlete at any sport, they work hard to get to where they are, but the Lord has blessed them with amazing talent. To the great leader who can inspire a group of people to accomplish amazing feats, God has granted you this ability.

If we are good at anything and in all our accomplishments, we are to give glory and honor to the Lord. The Lord warned the Israelites as he brought them out of captivity and into the promised land to guard themselves from thinking they came to the promised land by their own power: "Beware lest you say in your heart, 'My power and the might of my hand have gotten me this wealth'" (Deut. 8:17, ESV).

The Bible gives us many examples of lives from which we can learn. Job was a man of God who had much yet had it all taken away. God allowed Satan to take all that was valuable to Job, and he was brought to total despair. Later, the Lord restored him with even more than he had at the beginning. While Job was in the beginning stages of dealing with losing everything, his humility shined as he proclaimed, "Naked I came from my mother's womb, and naked shall I return. The LORD gave, and the LORD has taken away; blessed be the name of the LORD" (Job 1:21 ESV).

Consider the Brevity and Simplicity of Life

Have you ever stopped to consider how simple and short life is? When I ponder over the fragility of my body, the brevity of my life, and I consist of only the elements from the dirt—I am in awe of the majesty of God. I used to sit in chemistry class and stare at the periodic table. I knew nothing about the elements and was not interested at all, but I was amazed that everything on earth was derived from those elements. In reality, those elements are all that exists. How is that we have life? I am humbled knowing that our great Sustainer holds me together. As I think about these things, I am more and more convinced to surrender all to the One who gives me life!

Our forefather Abraham fully understood the gift of life. As he is making a request to God to not destroy the wicked city of Sodom and Gomorrah, he humbly makes the statement, "Since I have begun, let me speak further to my Lord, even though I am but dust and ashes" (Gen. 18:27, NLT). Abraham clearly understood he was speaking to the Creator who controls life and death. Abraham knew he came from the dust of the earth and his body will die turning into ash. This is a man of humility, understanding he is but dust in ashes yet put together by the very God he was petitioning.

Psalm 103 describes the brevity of life and the fragility of life:

> As a father shows compassion to his children, so the LORD shows compassion to those who fear him. For he knows our frame; he remembers that we are dust. As for man, his days are like grass; he flourishes like a flower of the field; for the wind passes over it, and it is gone, and its place knows it no more. (Ps. 103:13–16, ESV)

This is such an encouraging verse for me because we find here that God shows us compassion because he knows our frailty; he knows we are but dust. This verse also humbles me as I see how few my days actually are here on this earth. Even though we see flowers come and go with each year, this is how we are to the Eternal God.

Our time here on earth is very short. When we look at my days compared to the Eternal God, I am in awe.

When you look at our time here on this earth compared to history and the future, I do not see how people are arrogant. Seriously, in our history of the United States, presidents are the most powerful people in the country. I doubt I can name more than ten presidents right now. I am sure some academic person would think I'm an idiot, but in reality, why would I know more than ten? Our days are fleeting, and in one hundred years, all our worldly accomplishments will be meaningless. All that will matter are the eternal investments that we have made in the lives of those around us.

Psalm 90 addresses this same idea:

> For all our days pass away under your wrath;
> we bring our years to an end like a sigh. The
> years of our life are seventy, or even by reason
> of strength eighty; yet their span is but toil and
> trouble; they are soon gone, and we fly away.
> Who considers the power of your anger, and
> your wrath according to the fear of you? So
> teach us to number our days that we may get
> a heart of wisdom. (Ps. 90:9–12, ESV)

When we number our days two things happen: 1.) We are humbled in understanding our finite beings; and 2.) We learn to value each day since they are so few. As I ponder over life, I am humbled before the face of my Creator and Savior, Jesus Christ. I pray that each day I have on this earth is invested in his Kingdom and for his Glory!

O Lord: "Incline my heart to your testimonies, and not to selfish gain! Turn my eyes from looking at worthless things; and give me life in your ways" (Psalm 119:36–37 ESV).

God Hates Pride

As a football coach, I know I cannot stand players who think they know everything. If we are going to be any good, I need every single player to come out there and bring their talent and great attitudes, but I do not need them to come to practice thinking they know anything. I need them to do exactly what I tell them and be excited about doing it. When I have a team of guys thinking they know everything, it will be a miserable year.

You can't coach kids who have their own agenda and think they know everything. If I have a group of humble, talented kids, I bet our team wins the state championship. If I have a group of humble kids who aren't talented, it will be a fun year and we will win a bunch of games. But woe is me when I get a bunch of kids who think they know everything. I usually end the year wondering why God called me into coaching. It is unbearable. Even when we win, it is no fun coaching those kids.

Just as we can't coach kids with prideful hearts, God cannot either. For this reason, God hates pride, as we learn in his word: "Haughty eyes and a proud heart, the lamp of the wicked, are sin" (Prov. 21:4, ESV). We often forget that God is the author of life and he gives us the ability to do anything. We must humbly bow at the throne of his grace, seeking to do his will. We know nothing. We are lost in this sinful world. We are in desperate need of God's protection and security.

I often think about the NBA or NFL player when I think about how foolish pride is. The six-foot-one offensive lineman who has great skill, strength, and athleticism will never get drafted very high, if he even gets drafted at all. However the six-foot-six offensive lineman who has great skill, strength, and athleticism could end up a first-round draft pick and make a lot of money. Neither guy works harder than the other. (In reality, it's usually the six-foot-one guy who works harder.) God has blessed the one to be six feet six, and in our culture today, that can make him a lot of money in the game of football. Does he boast in his accomplishments? He should give God all the glory and use the platform God has allowed him to have and given him. To boast in his accomplishments is foolish!

I say the same thing for the great coach. I have had some great teams, and each one of those teams had great players. I have lost to coaches who have had less talent but were better coaches than me. I don't know if I am a good coach when it comes to all the details of coaching. I do know this: if I am good at anything, it is because God has given me the ability. When we win, it is because God has put good people around me, given me good players, and blessed the work of our hands. Do I look to glorify myself? No, I give God all the glory.

The Scoffer

I refer to the kids who think they know everything as scoffers. "Scoffer is the name of the arrogant, haughty man who acts with arrogant pride" (Prov. 21:24), as the Word says. These kids drive me nuts! Whenever a scoffer is around, there will be problems, and the Bible says to "drive out a scoffer, and strife will go out, and quarreling and abuse will cease" (Prov. 22:10, ESV). I write this and am convicted not to be the guy who needs to be driven out.

You cannot teach or instruct the scoffer, so "do not speak in the hearing of a fool, for he will despise the good sense of your words" (Prov. 23:9, ESV). A scoffer, fool, and mocker are all the same thing; you could tell this person the sky is blue, and they will argue. You cannot tell them anything, but "a scoffer does not like to be reproved; he will not go to the wise" (Prov. 15:12, ESV). They do not seek out wisdom, and they do not want to hear it. We are quick to label people scoffers, but we must make sure we are not becoming one ourselves.

God gives us warning to not be around these people in Psalm 1:

> Blessed is the man who walks not in the counsel
> of the wicked, nor stands in the way of sinners,
> nor sits in the seat of scoffers; but his delight is in
> the law of the LORD, and on his law he meditates
> day and night (Ps. 1:1–2, ESV).

As Christians, we just need to get away from the wicked, sinners, and scoffers. They are all the same thing. They will destroy us. We know that bad company corrupts good character. We must be very careful whom we allow to influence our minds. The people we talk with and associate with do have influence over us. If we subject our minds to the wicked, sinners, and scoffers, we will surely succumb to their influence over time.

As an adult, I have to guard myself from allowing the scoffer to influence me. As a coach, I must guard against the scoffer influencing my team. Some of my players could be scoffers; one of my coaches could be a scoffer; and some of my parents could be scoffers. These people think they know everything, and they do not get on board with the mission of the program. These people have to go, or they will destroy the program from the inside out. Satan has his people everywhere, and he will certainly try and destroy men who are trying to build for Jesus Christ. I do not care how great the player is, how good the coach is, or how important we think a certain parent may be—a scoffer must be driven out, and our trust must be in the Lord, not in man!

The Reward for Humility

As Champions for Jesus Christ, we are growing in our relationship with Christ every single day. As we grow in Christ we grow in humility. The more we know about Christ the less we think of ourselves. We will soon be saying of Christ with John the Baptist: "He must increase, but I must decrease" (John 3:30, ESV).

This probably does not sound like much of invitation as we witness to our unsaved friends. However, there is a reward for humility: "The reward for humility and fear of the LORD is riches and honor and life" (Proverbs 22:4 ESV). As we humble ourselves in the fear of the Lord and surrender all to him, we inherit all that is Christ's. In fact, we are brought in as heirs to the Kingdom of God. Not only are we saved from death and the wrath of God; we are given access to the Father and the Kingdom of God.

As sinful people our eyes are often veiled to the fact that life does not end when our earthly bodies die. Life is eternal. When the Bible talks of life, the reference is to our eternal state. When we humble ourselves before the Lord, we receive life in Christ forever more. There is no greater gift. This gift is so great it is hard for us to comprehend!

Humble in Victory

Anytime we have victory in our lives, we must pause and give thanks humbly before the Lord. He has given us the ability and the strength to have success. He is our Creator and Sustainer; we have life because he wills it. We have success because he allows it. How then can we take pride and become arrogant in success? The way to guard against this is to always look to Christ in victory.

When we win, we must realize that God has given us all the resources to be successful. He gives us bodies that work and minds that function. All are from him. At any point, this could be taken away. When the farmer has a great reaping season at harvest, did he bring the rain that made the produce grow? Did he provide the sunlight essential for growth? Yes, he worked and planned diligently. Yes, there is a ton of work to do at harvest to ensure all the produce is gathered. However, much of what led to his success he did not and could not do. The Lord blessed his crops. The glory must go to the Lord!

When we win, when we have success, we must point to the Lord as we acknowledge he is everything and we are nothing. We must not boast and present ourselves as haughty and arrogant to others. What is it that we take pride in? Our hard work? God grants the ability and desire to work hard. May we never let our minds ponder, *What great things my hands have done.* No! What great things our God has done! He is our strength.

God clearly tells us to not boast in our accomplishments or ourselves: "Let the one who boasts, boast in the Lord" (1 Cor. 1:31, ESV). He warns us of boasting with our own mouth: "Let another praise you, and not your own mouth; a stranger, and not your own lips" (Prov. 27:2, ESV). To the man who claims he is a self-made man, this is extremely foolish. We have breath because God wills it. None of us are self-made.

I enjoyed reading a story about how Roman generals would guard themselves from pride after they came home from conquering their enemy. As they were coming back from a victory and entering into the city where everyone was gathered to praise them, they would have someone whisper in their ear as they came back for victory, "All glory is fleeting." As thousands of people were chanting their names and glorifying these generals, the generals were wise enough to realize the moment will pass and they still had missions to carry out. Truly, all glory is fleeting, and tomorrow is a new day with new battles.

As Christians, we must understand if we desire and relish the praise of man, it can destroy our relationship with Jesus Christ. We were made to bring glory to Christ. Our lives are to be a living testimony of Christ, and we must always point to him. We were made to worship God. When we start to desire worship and praise from others, we will quit giving praise to the One to whom it is due. Therefore, always praise, honor, and point to God in all success—Humble in Victory!

Gracious in Defeat

Most often, in defeat, members of the team point the blame at each other. Coaches blame players and other coaches, players blame coaches, and parents blame coaches and other players besides their children. It is a giant excuse-making process. The worst part of defeat is seeing the opposing players and coaches hate and disrespect each other. If we are going to represent Christ, we must learn how to be gracious in defeat.

First and foremost, everyone on the team needs to be taught to take ownership of the loss. When a team loses, everyone is to be blamed; everyone could have done a little bit better in order to win. No one person can ever be blamed for a loss on the football field. From the coaches to the players, we all must take ownership and reflect upon what we could have done better to win. As a team, we treat each other with grace. If I am consumed with what I could have done better to win the game, how can it ever enter my mind what someone else did to cause us to lose?

Second, we must cross the field and shake the hand of the other team and submit ourselves to them, as they are the victors. As the head coach, I go over to the other head coach, and I congratulate him and I praise him for a great victory. I do not ever approach him with an aggravated or mad state of mind. I humble myself, submit to him as he is the victor, and I praise him. I'm trying to get to the point in my life where I can be joyful for the team and the coach who just beat us. (I don't know if this is possible, but I think it is right.)

Finally, as the head coach of my football team, everything is my fault. I can't blame a coach or a player for anything because as the coach, I allowed it to happen. If a player fumbles, then I didn't teach it well enough. If our guy misses a tackle, then I need to do a better job of teaching him how to tackle. Sure, I could make excuses, but no one wants to hear them. I will stand before my team and take the blame for the loss, eagerly seeking to correct all our mistakes as we move forward. I expect every person in our program to have this same attitude.

All of this might sound preposterous and even dumb. However, my goal in every circumstance God gives me is to represent Christ. (I do fail constantly, but it is always my goal to do right!) I want people to see Christ in my life, and I want to be a light for him at all times. On my own and in my flesh, there is no way I could submit to the other coach and praise him in his victory over me, much less be joyful for him. Praise God that it is no longer I who live but Christ who lives in me! By myself, without the power of Christ, I could never represent him. Apart from Christ, I am a prideful winner and a sore loser who is quick to blame everyone else for my failure. In Christ, I am Humble in Victory and Gracious in Defeat! Win or lose, to God be the glory.

A Prayer

O Lord, my Rock and my Strength. In you I lay my hope and my trust—you are my Hope and my Trust. Help me to die to my sinful self and my sinful desires, and may I live in Christ. May it be you who lives through me, and may I represent you at all times. Grant to me a humble heart, Lord. How could my heart grow prideful and arrogant when you have created all things? You are our Creator and our Sustainer. We have life because you will it. No man can make the rain fall or the sun rise. O Lord, without these simple things, we perish. Without Christ, we have no salvation and are hopeless. How can man boast? We are completely dependent upon you. Grant to me these things, Lord—a humble heart, a broken spirit, and may I tremble at your word. You are the Creator of all things, you are the Sustainer of all things, and you are the Redeemer of all things. If I boast of anything, Lord, may it be in Jesus Christ. Lead me, O Lord, may my life be a living testimony of Jesus Christ! Amen.

11

CREEPING SOFTNESS

THE ONE THING WE ALL better be careful to look out for is creeping softness.

When I talk of *softness*, I am not talking about physical prowess. The same linebacker who can lay a vicious lick on any given play can be the softest kid on the football team. *Softness* refers to one's lack of mental discipline. The mind controls the body. A strong man with a weak mind is soft. A physically weak man with a strong mind is tough. You do not have to be the strongest man to be the toughest guy in the weight room.

I constantly warn myself, players, and coaches of creeping softness. *Softness* is having no mental discipline and toughness; it is the inability to push oneself through a challenging situation. When we start to dwell on what we deserve and what we want, we are becoming soft. Softness can creep us and take over all of us. We will become excuse makers like we discussed in the "No Excuse" chapter.

Every coach in the world knows a team can have the best group of athletes in the world, but if they are mentally weak, they are going to lose when the going gets tough. When adversity strikes, they will surely falter. They cannot persevere through adversity because they are too busy blaming others instead of taking ownership and leading the way to victory. If we are to become all that God intended us to be, we must strive to make sure we do not let softness creep into our minds and bodies.

Satan is the master at whispering the word *can't* into our ears. When we start to believe and listen to these words, we become soft. I tell our players that when their minds start to whisper the word *can't*, this is a call to arms. It is time to battle. The devil is whispering lies into our ears. Do not believe those words. Fight against those words. Do not allow the devil to whisper softness into your mind. We can and we will push through by the power of Jesus Christ who works in us!

A Call to Strength

Unfortunately for us, we are all born in weakness. Sin is softness. We were born losers to sin. Therefore, we are naturally soft—imprisoned, defeated, and dead to sin. We are slaves to sin, and sinning is who we are and what we do. We cannot overcome sin on our own merit or by own power. This disease plagues us all, and there is no cure in and of ourselves. Sin is slowly killing us and we are headed toward a hopeless death. When it comes to sin, we are weak; we are soft.

But praise be to God who has sent his Son, Jesus Christ, to die on the cross for our sins. As Christians, our strength is not in and of ourselves but in our Lord and Savior, Jesus Christ. The world views being a Christian as soft and weak. How foolish this is. We all are soft and weak, as we have no answer for the death that awaits us all. Each day we move closer to this end. What is the answer? Is there any hope? Do we have any strength against the foe of death? We have an answer to death in Jesus Christ. This is strength the world will never know apart from Christ.

The Old Testament serves as great instruction for us in our lives as we read about the trials and struggles of the Israelites; we can learn from their mistakes and their successes. As God led the Israelites to the promised land, they were to trust in him completely. God was their source of power and strength. He told them many times they had only to trust in him and he would work for them and through them.

God was to be their source of power and strength. It is the same today for us. When the Israelites started relying on their own power and own strength, they quickly would become overwhelmed and dismayed with the task of conquering and overtaking the promised land. As they took their eyes off God, they would quickly become soft in their thinking. Their power and strength was God. They could never accomplish his mission by their own power. In fact, they would cower at the amazing feat of winning the promise land when they were focused on themselves.

In Deuteronomy, God gives a great warning to the Israelites to trust in him:

> "When you go out to war against your enemies, and see horses and chariots and an army larger than your own, you shall not be afraid of them, for the Lord your God is with you, who brought you up out of the land of Egypt. And when you draw near to the battle, the priest shall come forward and speak to the people and shall say to them, 'Hear, O Israel, today you are drawing near for battle against your enemies: let not your heart faint. Do not fear or panic or be in dread of them, for the Lord your God is he who goes with you to fight for you against your enemies, to give you the victory.'" (Deut. 20:1–4, ESV)

Fear, panic, and dread are all softness in the eyes of God. They are common to us, but God tells us to not fear. Why? We are to trust in him. He will work for us. Who is your strength and who is your power? Is it you? Do you trust in yourself and rely on your own power and strength? This will always fail you—if not in this life on earth, certainly in death. We are to trust completely in Christ. He is our strength and our power. He is our hope and our trust. He is the Creator of all things, the Savior of our souls. We are fools to not to rely on him for all things! We are soft on our own! We are strong in Christ!

Soft Christians

In Hebrews, the Bible gives us warning about becoming soft in our walk with the Lord: "Therefore we must pay much closer attention to what we have heard, lest we drift away from it" (Heb. 2:1, ESV). Once we become undisciplined in our daily pursuit of Jesus Christ, we will naturally start to drift. Instead of keeping our gaze upon the cross, we will start desiring the things of the world.

As a man, I must guard my heart against any type of lust. I pray daily that I will love and cherish my wife and only have eyes for her. As I keep my eyes upon Jesus Christ, I can do these things. However, I have met many men who have fallen out of love with their wives and have left their families. More often than not, what has happened is drifting away from the Lord. The man is called to be the spiritual leader in the household. The man has failed to lead, so not only has he drifted from Christ, his wife has drifted as well. The man has failed to make Christ supreme in his household. When we fail to keep our eyes on Christ, we lose the power to live a life pleasing to the Lord. All that is important to God and his kingdom crumbles in our life.

Remember we have defined *love* as sacrificial resolve to stay faithful and committed to a cause greater than self. So love is a choice. We are choosing to love someone. As in everything we do, our marriage should be rooted and grounded in Jesus Christ. As we keep our eyes on Jesus

Christ and are pursuing him, we are empowered by his Holy Spirit to live in him and for him. As men, God will also equip us with the power and the ability to lead our families in Jesus Christ. Heaven knows I am a gigantic failure in loving my wife as Christ commands, when left to my own power. If I am going to love her, serve her, cherish her, and remain faithful to her—it is the power of God that must work in me. There is no doubt I will fail and have failed on my own.

When I take my eyes off Christ, I will drift. This drifting is creeping softness. As I have mentioned earlier, softness breeds softness. The further we drift, the more lost we become. Soon our world will start to revolve around ourselves and not Christ. Our families and our wives will not be enough for us anymore. We will quickly fall into the lust of the flesh and its desires. Sin whispers through our bodies, and the devil whisper in our ears that we do not love our wives anymore and it is time to leave and find happiness. We deserve someone who will serve us. (And believe me, I bet my wife wants to leave me daily.) Sin tells us that it is not us who are called to serve but we are to be served. If you find yourself at this point—if I find myself at this point—softness has crept in and overtaken!

Whether you are in the midst of this, headed this way, or have already failed miserable in your past, the Lord promises to forgive us and restore us. We must understand this desire for change and something easier is our sin nature. It is against our nature to push forward and stay focused. We desire to serve ourselves and do whatever is necessary to make ourselves happy. Keeping our eyes on Christ and all that is important to him requires intense discipline.

This is just an example of how drifting can ruin what is so important to God and the gifts he has given us. There are many other scenarios of how sin will creep in and destroy our relationship with Christ and everything that is important to him. I used families as an example because our wives and our families are a gift from the Lord. They are the most important priority to God in the world. We must stand strong in Jesus Christ and lead!

Discipline Is the Antidote to Softness

From a football perspective, I define *discipline* as commanding your body to work when it does not want to work so that you may achieve your goals. We discussed how skipping a workout and a practice would help us skip that next workout. A bad attitude at practice will lead to poor work ethic at practice. A little bit of softness in you will soon make you completely soft. It will not take long. I tell the boys at 6:00 a.m. workouts that I have never once in my life enjoyed the sound of my alarm clock. I hate to wake up, and I'd like to throw the alarm clock at the wall every morning. It sure would be easy to turn it off and roll over; but I know if I do this, tomorrow, it will be easier to do it. We must command our bodies to do what it doesn't want to do!

In First Corinthians 10, the apostle Paul mentions how he must discipline his body and keep it under control in his quest to attain the imperishable wreath that is his in Christ Jesus:

> Do you not know that in a race all runners run,
> but only one receives the prize? So run that you
> may obtain it. Every athlete exercises self-control
> in all things. They do it to receive a perishable
> wreath, but we an imperishable. So I do not run
> aimlessly; I do not box as one beating the air. But
> I discipline my body and keep it under control,
> lest after preaching to others I myself should be
> disqualified. (1 Cor. 10:24–27, ESV)

If we are going to be effective for the kingdom of God, we must discipline ourselves. I believe the very first discipline we must learn is spending time with the Lord daily in prayer and Bible reading. We cannot overcome sin on our own power. It requires Christ. If we are diligent to pursue Christ daily, when temptation comes, we will have the answer—Jesus Christ.

How did Jesus defeat temptation? Scripture. In the Bible, Matthew 4 discusses Jesus being tempted by the devil. The devil tried to tempt Jesus through appealing to his human nature. Each time, Jesus answered the devil with scripture. Jesus was walking closely with God and pursuing him all of the day and night, so when tempted, he was quick to answer with scripture. He was ready. We must discipline ourselves to spend time with Christ daily so that every day—all day—we will be ready.

Even when we are walking closely with God and pursuing him, we still will have to be disciplined to make the right decisions. A great example is what is on our television screens. I am about to throw my TV away. If it were not for college football, I would have already done so. The TV offers us things to watch that are completely dishonoring to the Lord and feeds the lust and desires of our sin nature. This trash on TV is influencing the next generation, and that is scary. The sad thing is, even as Christians, we want to watch these shows.

If we are going to grow in holiness and godliness, we need to discipline ourselves to not allow unholy things into our minds, whether it be what we watch, what we listen to, or with whom we hang around. Sin is softness, and it will slowly creep up on us and destroy us. It is so subtle and so sneaky. Just like one practice turns into another missed practice, a bad show turns into a little bit worse show. We then start to desire the things we watch. We start to be okay with sin. We must guard ourselves against this. This requires discipline.

The Devil Whispers Lies

I was telling a boy about how rap music is trash and he shouldn't listen to it. I'm talking about the worldly rap music that is destroying people. For this particular person, I was talking about rap music because that is the stuff to which he allows influence over his mind. I'd say country, rock, or whatever other genres of music that do not point to Jesus Christ are trash as well. Could there be some good secular music? Who knows? For me, I'm going to guard my heart by the power of the Holy Spirit and not allow anything that is not Christ centered into my mind. I know my sin nature, and it is bad. I do not want to give it any food, not even a crumb!

So when I told this guy that the music he listens to poisons his mind, he responded back with this statement: "A wise man once told me that you can enjoy the music but just don't embrace the lifestyle." Of course, I pounced on that one and had a fun time doing so. A wise man told him that? How about a foolish man told him that. Man—a lie from the pit of hell! There is no way we can drink poison and not suffer from its damaging effects. This same wise man is basically saying this: "Go play with the lions but just don't let them bite." I've got no control over a lion biting me. And they most certainly will!

This wise man represents the whispers of the devil. He is always there enticing our sinful nature. He doesn't control us, but he entices us and tempts us with what he knows we want. "Do this, it won't hurt you," he says. Oh, how our sin nature loves to hear these false promises. It is so appealing to us when Satan and his host of demons whisper to us that sin will not destroy us. He is lying!

This whispering in our ear is an enticement to sin. The devil knows when sin increases, it never decreases. Sin breeds sin. Softness breeds softness. The music out in the world, no matter the genre, is appealing to our sin nature. If we subject our minds to it, we will surely fall prey to the sin it endorses. We must be on guard against this creeping sinfulness, creeping softness, as thought to us by the Lord: "Keep your heart with all vigilance for from it flows the springs of life" (Prov. 4:23, ESV).

Training Requires Discipline

I keep waiting for the day when making godly and wise decisions is easy. In the weight room, I like to say, "If it is easy, you aren't doing it right." Making wise decisions can be painful but beneficial. When I first get the eighth and ninth graders doing squats, they absolutely loathe squat day. Squats are hard, and they can make the muscles ache. Besides power cleans, there is not a better lift in the weight room for developing power than squats. Squats stress the entire body. They are hard. About 95 percent of kids do not want to do squats!

However, as they grow older, they start to see the value in squats and how it makes them more explosive athletes. As they see the value it provides, they approach squat day with a different mentality. They still do not desire to do a squat for how it will make them feel, but they do them eagerly, knowing the value they will gain in their athletic development. They grow to embrace squats as a tool to get them what they desire—being more explosive.

I think this is exactly what happens as we grow in Christ. It's not that we don't desire sin if we embrace the desires of the flesh. However, we understand the value of pursuing godliness and holiness. Sometimes it's hard for my wife and I to quit watching the show that we enjoy, but since the show prompts unholiness in our thought life, we must turn the show off. There are many things we will want to do that are not edifying for us.

Through the discipline of saying *no* to sin and, therefore, pursuing holiness, we are training ourselves for godliness. The Bible says, "Rather train yourself for godliness; for while bodily training is of some value, godliness is of value in every way, as it holds promise for the present life and also for the life to come" (1 Tim. 4:7–8, ESV).

I wish the apostle Paul had used a different word than *train*. Training requires physical and mental discipline. Like squats, it can be painful. I wish it were easy. Growing in holiness and godliness is not easy! The easy choices lead to softness; the hard choices help grow us in holiness and godliness!

Leading for Christ Requires Discipline

If one is not disciplined in his own life, how will he ever lead men? Make no mistake—we are all leaders of men. God has called us to be salt and light in this world. Whether we are directly leading men in our jobs or not, we are all to lead men for Jesus Christ. You can say that you don't have a leadership personality, and I'll say that makes no sense. Moses told the Lord the same thing. We can lead by our attitudes and actions. We are to put on Christ. When we put on Christ, he will lead through us!

Here are a few thoughts on the value of discipline as we lead for Jesus Christ. I have followed this up with a prayer to the Lord to help us be men of discipline:

- Making good choices requires discipline.
- Resolve and fortitude require discipline.
- Studying requires discipline.
- Not griping and not complaining requires discipline.
- Eating correctly requires discipline.
- Exercising requires discipline.
- Daily quiet times with the Lord require discipline.
- Managing money requires discipline.
- Managing time requires discipline.
- Choosing a good attitude requires discipline.
- Humility requires discipline.
- Loving, serving, desiring, and loyalty to our wives require discipline.
- Dating appropriately before marriage requires discipline.
- Not having sex before marriage requires discipline.
- Commitment requires discipline.
- Executing properly requires discipline.
- Follow through requires discipline.

A Prayer

My God and my King, my Savior—how great you are! How majestic is your name in all the earth. Lord, I desire to become like you. I want to grow in holiness, godliness, and righteousness. I desire to be able to say along with the apostle Paul, "Imitate me, as I imitate Christ." However, Lord, I feel my sinful nature always at war with this desire to be like you. This sinful nature is softness creeping and dwelling in me. O Lord, help me to mortify the flesh and its desires. Help me to be strong and powerful in Christ.

Lord, I know I must train myself to destroy the desires of the flesh and put on Christ daily. Training requires discipline. Help me to discipline my body and bring it under control so Christ may reign unhindered in my body. Help me to put to death the sin nature in me. This is no easy task. In fact, this task cannot be accomplished under my own power. I have no power over sin and am enslaved to it. But you, Lord, you have conquered sin, and it has no power over you. In your grace and mercy, you have given us the ability to abide in you. You promise to fill us with your Holy Spirit and it no longer be I who live but Christ who lives in me. We can overcome and conquer sin by the power of Jesus Christ living and moving in us. We have been forgiven for our sins by the blood of Jesus Christ.

O Lord, grant to me discipline in my quest to be a leader for Jesus Christ. May I only pursue the virtue of discipline because I want to bring you glory and honor. I want and desire to be a man for Jesus Christ. This is no easy road. The soft man will never make it. We are all soft apart from you. You are Strength and Power. You are my Rock and my Shield. You are my Hope and my Trust. My life is yours. Help me to mortify the flesh and live a life wholly in Jesus Christ. Amen.

12

BE A CHAMPION

WE ARE CHAMPIONS WHEN WE surrender all to this world and pursue Christ with all of our hearts, all of our souls, all of our minds, and with all of our strength. The Word teaches us, "And you shall love the Lord your God with all your heart and with all your soul and with all your mind and with all your strength" (Prov. 12:30, ESV). A Champion will lay aside all selfish desires and pursuits of glory in this world and live for Jesus Christ. A Champion has one focus and one mission—to bring glory and honor to Jesus Christ through growing to become more and more like him. As we grow in Jesus Christ, we will reflect him more and more. His character will become our character. This pursuit to be like Christ leads us to become Champions.

The world crowns its champions with perishable trophies and offers them fleeting glory and praise of man. Pursuing these trophies is fun. I like to win and do not like to lose. There is fun in preparing to be the best. We can be in pursuit of winning a worldly trophy. But this cannot be the reason we exist. The pursuit of this worldly trophy cannot become our identity. We must be careful that the pursuit of perishable trophies does not become our idol. We must guard our hearts against the desire for the praise of man. All of it is going to pass away, just like us.

Jesus Christ was the only real Champion this world has ever seen. We all have a common enemy, and it is called sin and death. Not one of us will ever stand victorious over sin and death. We will be defeated. But, praise God, Jesus Christ has conquered death and he stands as the Champion! Through his blood and his sacrifice, God has imparted his victory over death to us. All we have to do is accept him as Lord and surrender all to him. We can be Champions over death and sin through Christ.

I pray what I am saying makes sense to you. Do you see we are victorious through Jesus Christ? He is the Champion as he has come and freed us from slavery to sin and provided a path to eternal life. Man, winning a state or national championship is a big deal, but defeating death? Do we understand the significance of this? Do you see how Jesus Christ is *the* Champion? Nothing compares. Everything else is fleeting. This Championship is eternal. It lasts forever. He is the Champion. He is our model.

I define "being a Champion" as surrendering all to Christ; accepting him as our Lord and Savior; and then pursuing him with all our heart, our souls, our minds, and with all our strength. As he came to this earth for us, he accomplished three things: (1) he conquered death; (2) he paid the price for our sins, and our sins are forgiven as we face the wrath of God for sinning against him; and (3) we are no longer separated from God as we are reunited with the Father through the blood of Jesus Christ.

Christ is the Champion. He has imparted the rights of his Championship to us through his grace. Therefore, we are Champions when we surrender all of ourselves and pursue him with all of our might!

Champions in Christ

What an amazing God we have. Along with Adam and Eve, we have rejected God since the beginning of time. However, through God's grace and mercy, he sent his Son, Jesus Christ, to die for our sins. Jesus Christ willingly came down to earth to pay the penalty for our sins. Someone had to pay the price for our sins. We certainly could not because God required a perfect sacrifice. Man is sinful and the opposite of a perfect sacrifice. Before Christ, we stood defeated and hopeless.

In the sports world, we can understand this idea of hopelessness. You see programs all the time that are so mired in mediocrity and failure there is nothing those individuals can do to get out of it. They are so defeated, they do not even think about victory. It is a lost cause. This usually leads to a further decline. You see bad programs become worse. This is exactly how man's state is apart from Christ—defeated and hopeless.

Christ, counting himself as insignificant, humbly came to earth to live the perfect life so he could become the perfect sacrifice. What a picture of grace and mercy. The Lord of lords and King of kings willingly came down to earth where he was rejected and mocked to live the perfect life so he can be the perfect sacrifice for a people who have rejected him.

In our sin state, we are totally evil and totally depraved. There is no good in us as "none is righteous, no, not one; no one understands; no one seeks for God" (Rom. 3:10, ESV). Since sin entered this world, we lost access to the God and no longer walk with him or can approach him. We seek our own way, and our own interests are all that is important. We are self-centered and self-righteous. We are lost. We are blind. We believe that this earth is all that there ever was and all that there ever will be. We do not seek God, we do not understand we are sinners, and, therefore, salvation from sin does not even enter into our minds. We don't care about a savior, and we aren't looking for one!

Does it make any sense that Jesus Christ would come to save a people like this? Absolutely not! But this should cause us to overflow with rejoicing and praise. God looked down and saw a people who were totally lost and depraved. Through his grace and mercy, he sent

Jesus Christ to become our Champion against death and sin. Through the work of Jesus Christ, we have gone from being a completely lost and depraved people to a people who have power and strength. We have victory over eternal death, wrath, and sin through the blood of Jesus Christ. We now have access to the Father through the blood of Jesus Christ. All this is Victory.

I wish I could correlate some type of worldly victory with the victory we have in Jesus Christ. It is impossible! If you do not understand this Victory, I pray the Lord will open your eyes to his Victory. For those who understand the Victory, I pray you will continue to grow in Jesus Christ and lead for him. When God opens our eyes to the salvation we have in Jesus Christ, nothing else in this life matters. We see we have been created for a much higher purpose. From men and women who sought after worldly championship, we become men and women who desire to become Champions for Jesus Christ!

Living as a Champion

As Champions in Christ, God has called each of us to live for his glory and his honor. Our lives are to reflect him. Through the power of the Holy Spirit living in us, we must be lights for Jesus Christ in this world. In all that we do and all the activities we undertake, there must be a central purpose—Jesus Christ. The sport you play, the subject you study, the community service project you perform, the instrument you play, whatever it is you do, must be done for the glory of the Lord. "And whatever you do, in word or deed, do everything in the name of the Lord Jesus, giving thanks to God the Father through him" (ESV), we read in Colossians 3:17.

When I surrendered all to Christ by the miraculous work of the Holy Spirit in my life, God convicted me that everything I do was to be for him. As a coach, I found the following verse and I wrote it everywhere: "Unless the Lord builds the house, those who build it labor in vain" (Ps. 127:1, ESV). This was a clear directive to me that

I was to focus solely on building a football program for the glory of God. This verse made it clear that even if I work my tail off and build the best program in the country, if I do it for any other reason than Christ, it is vanity!

I know the Lord has used Psalm 127:1 to help direct me to understanding the mission I have as a football coach to build Champions for Jesus Christ. I'm not focused on building a worldly champion. Yes, we work our tails off to be our absolute best. Yes, we want to win championships. But it is not the reason we exist! Christ is the reason. He is our purpose and is the foundation of our program. When I die and stand before the Lord, he will not ask me how many games I won. He will be concerned with the work I did for his kingdom. Therefore, by the power of the Holy Spirit that lives within me, I build for the Lord!

Whatever it is you are doing at this moment, God has placed you there. You are to live as a Champion in order that you may be a light for Jesus Christ. I know for the players I coach, being a Champion requires them to pursue Christ with all their hearts, give perfect effort in the classroom, and be respectful of their teachers. They are to be leaders for Christ among their classmates. They are to honor their father and mother. When they practice, they are to practice hard; when they lift weights, they are to lift hard. When they get on the field on Friday nights, they are to give everything they have for the glory of God. Their play and attitude should speak volumes about whose they are (Jesus Christ's). They are to set the proper example. God will use their desire to be a Champion for Christ!

What we have to understand is, there is no blueprint for being a Champion for Jesus Christ in a particular field. God will take a heart that has been surrendered to him and mold and shape it. He will lead and guide us as we pursue him with all our hearts and souls. He will build the house. He will show us the way. Seek him and trust in him. As we desire to become Champions for Jesus Christ, he is our power and strength.

What Does a Champion for Christ Look Like?

Over the years coaching, I have incorporated character building into all parts of our program. The whole goal is to produce the character of Jesus Christ in our players. Our coaches are responsible for leading in the process in these character traits. I want to share them with you and I hope you can use these in your pursuit of becoming a champion.

The words have a double meaning. My prayer is that God is using the coaching staff to lay a foundation for Jesus Christ in these boys. As we teach them to be Warriors on the field we are also teaching them to be Champions for Jesus Christ in all they do.

1. We Will Play FASTER

This philosophy represents the way our football players will play the game. Each letter stands for a specific word. The word correlates to how each player must play and guides the coaches to what is important. Each word we select must be able to be used to make us a better football team and also correlate with our pursuit of Christ. The words have a double meaning. My prayer is that God is using the coaching staff to lay a foundation for Jesus Christ in these boys. As we teach them to be Warriors on the field, we are also teaching them to be Champions for Jesus Christ in all they do.

We. We are a team. (In each other category, *we* means the same thing.) No one is more important to the team. We are group of men who die to our sinful, selfish agenda and pursue playing for great love of one another. Should the kingdom of God look any different?

FASTER. We want to play fast. This has to do with the tempo in which we practice and play but, more importantly, the intensity we must maintain. We must fly to the football to make tackles and give great effort in our execution on the football field. In the same way, we must maintain our intensity in our pursuit of Jesus Christ.

Fanatical. A fanatic is someone consumed to the point of obsession with something. We will be fanatical in the details of the game. Players will be fanatics in their execution, and coaches will be fanatical in coaching every detail. We must be fanatics as Christians. Jesus instructs us in the Bible how our outward actions cannot be all that matters. What about the desires of our heart? He tells us that if our eyes cause us to sin, then get rid of them. This is fanatical. He isn't saying to cut our eyes out; rather, if that TV show is causing you lust, quit watching it. If your computer is a catalyst to your addiction to pornography, then go throw it in the trashcan. Be fanatical in your quest to be holy!

Attack. We don't want to sit back and let the other team dictate to us what they are going to do. We are going to have a plan and attack every single play. As Christians, we must attack life. We cannot let life happen to us but must be intentional in all we do for the glory of Jesus Christ.

Simple. We don't want to make football overcomplicated. The game is hard enough in and of itself with the physical demands. We want to do a few things and do them really well. I believe the Christian walk is the same. We must surrender all, keep our eyes focused on Jesus Christ, and seek him daily.

Tough. We don't want mentally weak kids. Toughness has nothing to do with physical strength and everything to do with mental strength. Tough kids are disciplined. We train toughness daily. Being a Champion for Jesus Christ requires mental toughness. I must discipline my body and my mind and keep my eyes on the cross. It takes effort! It is hard. The weak-minded man will never be a Champion for Jesus Christ. In our own power, we can't! Our strength and power is in Christ.

Execute. Everyone has an idea on how to win; few are willing to pay the price and demand excellence in the execution. We will strive for perfection in our execution. The Bible tells us that God looks at the intentions of our hearts. We must desire to be perfect in our execution of his law and commands. We will fall way short, but we must work for perfect execution.

Relentless. We will give perfect effort in our pursuit to be our very best. We will play with relentless passion and desire. From a football perspective, we will pursue the football with relentless passion and desire. We will block until the whistle blows with relentless desire. Everything we do will be with relentless passion! As Christians, we must be relentless in our pursuit of Jesus Christ. I am not preaching work's righteousness, but we must give great effort in our quest to grow in Jesus Christ. For his glory and his honor, we exist. We are made in his image. We would be fools to not relentlessly pursue him. This is our purpose.

2. We Will Work HARDER

This motto goes with our year-round athletic development program. Not only are we training the body in hopes of our kids becoming great athletes, but also more importantly, we are training the toughness of their minds.

HARDER. I always tell the parents of our players that a major goal of mine is to teach their kids how to work hard. I don't define working hard as showing up one day for three hours. I define working hard as being committed each day, consistently showing up, and working with intensity. We must pursue our relationship with this mind-set. Each day, we must be committed to Christ and consistently pursue Christ with intensity. As a coach, I want each kid to grow as an athlete. As Christians, it is imperative that we are seeking Christ and growing more and more like him daily.

Hard work. We will work hard in our quest to be the very best we can be, physically and mentally. God gave each of us different talents and abilities. All that matters is the effort we give in developing the talent and then using the talent he has given us. As we pursue to become more and more like Christ, it is no easy task. We live in a sinful and fallen world, and to put on Christ daily takes effort! To lay everything aside in this world and keep our eyes on Christ takes work on our end.

There is no easy formula. We must be willing to work. The Christian walk requires discipline and effort. These are work words!

Attitude. One of the very few things we control in life is our attitude. Our attitude will determine our effectiveness. If the boys show up to develop as athletes and they have a bad attitude, they are wasting my and their time. I love the saying "The man who thinks he can and the man who thinks he can't are both right." I wake up each morning, and I have to make myself believe today is an opportunity to get better. When we are seeking and growing in Christ, our attitudes are fruitful. When I am pursuing Christ with all my heart, my attitude is great because it is Christ who is living and working in me. When I neglect to pursue Christ daily, my flesh starts to take over and my attitude turns for the worst!

Respect. A respectful person is a humble person. They look at others and value their opinions and ideas. A respectful person is a coachable person. As a coach, I want to demand respect from our players while working to earn their respect. As Christians, do we respect that the Bible is the word of God? Are we humble enough to accept his instruction and know that God's way is best? We must humble ourselves and learn to love and treasure the word of God. We must respect the word of God and God's authority in our lives.

Discipline. Discipline is commanding your body to work when it does not want to work so that you may achieve your goals. Our players must discipline themselves daily to show up and work out with a great attitude. This requires discipline. Our walk with Christ requires discipline. Choosing to spend time with him, choosing to make the right decision, and choosing to flee temptation and sin are very hard things to do. We must train ourselves in discipline.

Excellence. Excellence is seeking to bring God glory and honor by giving perfect effort to become your absolute best with the talent God has given you in *all* that God has called you to do. Our players must seek excellence in the effort they give, the form they use in their lifts, and in how they motivate and encourage one another. Just like in our Christian walk, they will fail and make mistakes. However, excellence is getting back up and striving to become more. Is the Christian walk any different? We must pursue excellence as we live for Jesus Christ.

Resilience. We must persevere in our quest to become mentally and physically tough. We will fall. We will make mistakes. But we will never quit! Our Christian walk will be laced with failure and challenges. However, we must never give in! The devil is always there whispering in our ear, "You can't. Why try? Give up!" Through the power of the Holy Spirit living and working in us, we will persevere.

3. We Strive for HUMILITY

Even though we incorporate a character trait into every letter, this motto is intentionally developed for character training. I want humble players and coaches who embody the characteristics described. I work daily to embody these characteristics described. As your read these traits, just imagine if everyone with whom you worked embodied these. I must admit, as I wrote these, I was convicted of how far I fall short!

HUMILITY. Arrogance is the opposite of humility. We cannot coach an arrogant kid whose whole world revolves around himself or herself. I pray that God would make our players humble so we can coach them. The very first thing God does in salvation is, he reveals to us our prideful and arrogant ways. We cannot become Champions for Jesus Christ until we are humbled and willing to get on our knees and surrender our life to him.

Honest. I always tell our parents that if they think their child does not lie to them, they are insane! We all lie, or we all want to lie. This is just our sin nature. We are born liars, and we will always lie, apart from Jesus Christ. We must first understand this. Honesty is very important in all aspects, especially teamwork. Even if we do wrong, it is important to be honest. I love talking to my offensive lineman after our quarterback got sacked. I'll say, "What happened, whose man was that?" Most of the time, I get confirmation from each offensive lineman that it was not their man. They lie because they are embarrassed. This destroys my ability to fix the protection problem. We must tell the truth!

As the Lord opens our eyes to his wondrous truth, we are faced with our sinful ways and must be truthful with ourselves. I am a sinner, and I am in desperate need of a savior. In my flesh, I am a liar, a cheat, and a dirty scoundrel. This is the hard truth. Praise the Lord for sending Jesus Christ to die on the cross for my sins. Praise the Lord for sending his Holy Spirit to live in me that I may die to my sinful ways and live in Christ.

Unselfish. There is no room for selfish players on a championship football team. Any team that has selfish players, no matter how good the player is, their season will end sooner than it should. As we die to our sinful selves and Christ comes into our lives to enable us to be Champions for Christ, the very first conviction we have is to die to our selfish agenda and seek to serve and work well with others. Death to self and life in Christ!

Merciful. What a weak word right? Wrong! We must be men and women who show grace and mercy, men and women who care about others. As we die to ourselves and our personal agendas, we will look and see there are people we need to love and encourage every single day. The merciful man does not just help those who can help him; he looks and desires to serve the weak and the hopeless in order that Christ may be exalted. This is what Christ did for us. We were lost and hopeless, heading toward death and eternal wrath. Christ, in his mercy, saved us. Mercy requires great strength and discipline.

Integrity. I've heard integrity as doing the right thing when no one is watching. The problem with this definition is the world's version of *right* is "anything that benefits the self." *Integrity* is a heart that is fully committed to Christ and follows his ways, no matter the time, place, or circumstance.

Loyal. Everyone in our world is looking to use people to gain something in this world. People praise one another most of the time because they are looking for something. Loyalty, to me, is being genuine, being real. Christ is the example of loyalty as he faithfully fulfilled his mission: "Even as the Son of Man came not to be served but to serve, and to give his life as a ransom for many" (Matt. 20:28, ESV).

Intent. I like to use the word *intentional.* We should have purpose and intent in all that we do. As a football coach, it is imperative that every single thing we do at practice is planned and scripted. If not, I will just whimsically make the kids do things that have no meaning or value. As Christians, we need to be intentional in making Christ the reason we do all that we do. Christ is all things—he is science; he is math; he is life! He is my football team. Nothing exists apart from God; therefore, we must be intentional in making him central in everything we say and do.

Thankful. It is in our sinful nature to expect things to be done for us. We also think the whole world should revolve around us! Do you know that some kids thank me for coaching them? I want their parents to write a book so I can raise my son to be like them. *Wow!* As Christians, we need to spend time developing the character trait of thankfulness. The lyrics of the song, "Thank You, Lord, for Saving My Soul" written by missionaries Seth and Bessie Sykes, are flying in my mind. Oh, how the Lord could transform our souls if we started off the day proclaiming these lyrics:

> Thank You, Lord, for saving my soul,
> Thank You, Lord, for making me whole;
> Thank You, Lord, for giving to me
> Thy great salvation so rich and free.

Yielding. I don't think anyone can ever be a good employee until they can put their personal agenda and thoughts aside and yield to authority. I know for sure they can't be good members of a football team. Once again, yielding has everything to do with being humble. I can be a team player when I yield to the greater good of the team. If I am to be effective for Christ, I must yield my desires and wants in this world and live for Christ. I must yield every desire I have to the greater good of the kingdom. I must pray that my desires are in line with Christ's desires.

4. We Become WARRIORS

The goal of our football program is to build Champions for Jesus Christ. We are working to instill character values that will enable these young men to grow to be faithful husbands, loving fathers, and leaders in their communities for Christ. The finished product hopefully is a Warrior, a man who is ready to go out and take on the world. At the very least, I hope to have laid a foundation for Jesus Christ. Many of them are not Warriors for Christ when they leave me but I know that the seed has been planted, and in God's timing, he will make it grow. I pray with great diligence, they leave us with the characteristics we teach as they leave our program.

WARRIOR. Our mission is to create Champions for Jesus Christ. God has called us to help equip the young men he has put under us with the ability to go out into the world and be leaders for Christ. I like to think that after four years in our football program, our boys have been taught about the fight and war that is going on in the spiritual realm for man's soul. They devil is "prowling around like a roaring lion seeking someone to devour" (1 Pet. 5:8, ESV). We cannot just sit back and let him destroy us. We must be Warriors. This takes work.

Wise. I hope all my players make straight As and graduate tops in their classes. However, this does not make one wise. Wisdom is knowledge and insight into Jesus Christ's desires for our life. The practical application of wisdom in life is discernment, discretion, and prudence. Our athletic director always tells everyone to make wise decisions. If they are not seeking the Lord and not walking with him, they will never make wise decisions. We can never choose wisdom apart from Christ. We must seek wisdom; we must pursue wisdom. As we pursue wisdom, we will then find ourselves making wise decisions.

Accountable. Every decision we make in our lives will impact other people. In football, we have taught the boys to be accountable to one another. If one person makes a mistake, it impacts the entire team. As a Christian, I must be accountable to God. I must seek to follow his ways and his commands. He has given us laws and commands for our benefit and well-being. Every law, command, statute, and rule he has ever given is perfect and good. I must also be accountable to my family. My relationship with my wife and my devotion to her will surely impact my children. The only things we have that are of any eternal value are the souls God has placed under our care.

Responsible. I am responsible for my actions. In our football team, we do not allow players to make excuses and blame others. We win together and we lose together. Each of us is responsible for our actions. We want to teach our boys to show up on time, to work hard, and to love and respect one another. This is being responsible. Being responsible leads to trust. A group of people who love each other and trust each other will accomplish amazing feats. We need young men who will grow up and be responsible for their families, their communities, and the church.

Reliable. I am going to coach and invest in the boys who will show up and work each day with a great attitude. They can't miss practice and expect to get better. They can't come to practice feeling sorry for themselves and have a productive day. Each day is a blessing and an opportunity as "this is the day that the Lord has made; let us rejoice and be glad in it" (Ps. 118:24, ESV). When we approach each day with this attitude, we prove reliable to all of those around us.

Industrious. This is a great word for hard work. I expect my players, coaches, and myself to show up with a great attitude and a strong work ethic. Working hard is a virtue. We want to be great at what we do—we want to grow in Christ, we want to get stronger, but we do not want to work. Everybody wants and desires to be successful; few are willing to pay the price. I believe this virtue will take these young men far as they strive to be faithful husbands and loving fathers. Both of these require hard work. However, they are the two most important priorities in the eyes of Jesus Christ.

Obedient. There is nothing I love more than when I tell a player something, he responds with a "Yes, sir," or "No, sir." The boys know I love them; but I tell them that when we are on that football field, I could be dead wrong, but they better react to me as I am right. If I am wrong, I will apologize later. Don't we often argue with God about some of his rules or our situation in life? When we start to question God, we are not far from falling into egregious sin. We must strive for obedience. Obedience requires trust and humility. We humble ourselves before God and trust him because he is our Creator, Sustainer, and Savior!

Respectful. Being respectful means showing everyone honor around us. It is counting oneself as insignificant and serving others. It is being thankful for everything we have. As a coach, I need to work hard to love and encourage my players in order to earn their respect. However, the players should respect me because I am the head coach. Respect works both ways. I respect my headmaster because he is my boss, and I will do what he demands without question. I believe as we show people respect, we will earn favor in their eyes. We want to grow in favor with man just as Jesus did, as we read in the Word: "And Jesus increased in wisdom and in stature and in favor with God and man" (Luke 2:52, ESV).

Servant. This is the most important part of any WARRIOR. We are striving to be men who imitate Jesus Christ. Jesus Christ came "not to be served but to serve, and to give his life as a ransom for many" (Matt. 20:28, ESV). We cannot serve until we humble ourselves and count others as more important. We would have an amazing football team if no player had any agenda other than to serve the brother who fights beside him. Every man serving the great interest of the other is a picture of the kingdom of God. It is a picture of how the church should look.

Trust in the Champion—Jesus Christ

Every Friday, game day, I send out a devotional to our parents. I briefly talk about the upcoming opponent and then, prayerfully, present a message that points to Jesus Christ. Football is intertwined just like in this book, and I know winning is on everyone's mind. I always sign off the email with the parting verse: "The horse is made ready for battle, but victory belongs to the Lord" (Prov. 21:31, ESV).

As a football team, it is our responsibility to develop the best process and then work our tails off to execute. We are responsible for our hard work and diligence. This is preparing the horse of battle. It is a great verse to go along with our "Win the Day" philosophy. We must do everything in our power to win. However, we are not in control of the outcome.

God is sovereign and in control of all things. He controls who wins and who loses. Victory belongs to the Lord. We can trust that God is in absolute control of all things. When it comes to winning and losing football games, I do not believe God is too concerned about the game. However, he is concerned about his people who are coaching and playing in it.

Just as it is my job to develop a game plan to win and challenge our players to work hard in the pursuit of winning, we are responsible for pursuing Jesus Christ. God's will for us is that we grow in Jesus Christ and become more like him. We must be diligent in our daily walk with him. We are not righteous through our commitment to growing in Christ; this only comes from the blood of Jesus Christ. However, God does require us to desire him and to pursue him.

Just like worldly victories are from God, much more so are our spiritual victories. The desire to pursue Christ is given to us by God. The growth in Christ is through the work of the Holy Spirit. We are both responsible to work, but we must trust and understand that it is the work of God when we actually grow in Jesus Christ.

God never promises to give us worldly victories. He does promise that He will grow us in Christ. We often learn a lot through adversity. Never blame God for a loss—thank him for the trials that shape and mold us more into his image. Praise God when you can look back on your life and see growth in him. For this is the work of God. Victory belongs to the Lord!

The Pursuit of the Championship

How on the face of the earth can we measure up to God's standards? You and I can't! This is always what amazes me about Jesus Christ. He was the perfect sacrifice—meaning, he did not sin! Our righteousness will never be through our works and our effort; it will always be through the blood of Jesus Christ. However, even though we cannot be perfect, we are to strive to be perfect. God watches the motives of our heart. We will fail daily, but the righteous man continues to get back up and strive for excellence. The Bible teaches us, "The godly may trip seven times, but they will get up again" (Prov. 24:16, NLT).

I challenge you and myself to take to heart Paul's words in Philippians about pursuing Christ:

> Not that I have already obtained this or am already perfect, but I press on to make it my own, because Christ Jesus has made me his own. Brothers, I do not consider that I have made it my own. But one thing I do: forgetting what lies behind and straining forward to what lies ahead, I press on toward the goal for the prize of the upward call of God in Christ Jesus. (Phil. 3:12–14, ESV)

Just like Paul, we must press on toward the prize. We must set our gaze upon Jesus Christ and surrender all to him. We will fail often in our pursuit of excellence in Christ. But we must always get back up through the power of Jesus Christ and press on. We must give everything we have in our quest to become a champion in Jesus Christ. Our championship is when we will stand before the Lord and hear the words, "Well done, good and faithful servant" (Matt. 25:23, ESV).

A Prayer

How great you are, O God. You are my Strength, my Rock, and my Salvation. In you, I place my hope and my trust. Teach me what being a true Champion is Lord. This world has all kinds of enticing offers and desires, but they all end in death. They are passing away—here today and gone tomorrow. Lord, help me to keep my eyes focused upon you and living for you; the power to do so resides in you. We can only be Champions in the world by fixing our eyes upon you and surrendering all to you.

Teach me about being a Champion for Christ. Keep me from creating worldly idols here on earth. Everything you have created is good and has value but only when you are at the center of it. When we go off and pursue worldly victory and championships apart from you, we will become separated from you. Separation from you leads to death. O Lord, we can gain the whole world and in the process lose our souls. Lord, we can lose everything here on this earth and gain eternal life!

Lord, I know you call us to excellence and to strive to work hard in everything we do. There is nothing wrong with desiring and working to be our best, as long as you are central in the process. Guard my heart, O Lord. May my heart's desire always be to become a Champion for Jesus Christ and not a champion for my own glory; there is a distinct difference.

O Lord, I will give my all in pursuit of you. I will serve you with all my heart, all my soul, and all my mind. I will give my all here on this earth in what you have called me to do for your glory and your honor. I do not work hard and labor to build my own empire where I can be exalted by this world. Rather, I work hard and labor for your kingdom so that you may be exalted. Help me to be a reflection of you. Make me a Champion for Jesus Christ!

CPSIA information can be obtained
at www.ICGtesting.com
Printed in the USA
BVHW031725260219
541082BV00048B/694/P